P9-DMI-523

"You're Grounded!"

MASHPEE PUBLIC LIBRARY
PO BOX 657
MASHPEE MA 02649

"You're Grounded!"

✦

How to Stop Fighting and Make the Teenage Years Easier

A Teenage Perspective

Vanessa Van Petten

A Book by a Teen
For Teens and Their Parents

iUniverse, Inc.
New York Lincoln Shanghai

"You're Grounded!"
How to Stop Fighting and Make the Teenage Years Easier

Copyright © 2007 by Vanessa Van Petten

All rights reserved. No part of this book may be used or reproduced by any means, graphic, electronic, or mechanical, including photocopying, recording, taping or by any information storage retrieval system without the written permission of the publisher except in the case of brief quotations embodied in critical articles and reviews.

iUniverse, Inc.

iUniverse books may be ordered through booksellers or by contacting:

iUniverse
2021 Pine Lake Road, Suite 100
Lincoln, NE 68512
www.iuniverse.com
1-800-Authors (1-800-288-4677)

The views expressed in this work are solely those of the author and do not necessarily reflect the views of the publisher, and the publisher hereby disclaims any responsibility for them.

ISBN: 978-0-595-43875-4 (pbk)
ISBN: 978-0-595-68334-5 (cloth)
ISBN: 978-0-595-88198-7 (ebk)

Printed in the United States of America

"Step back mainstream self-help books, there is a new genre taking over book-shelves nationwide. *You're Grounded* by Vanessa Van Petten tackles the infamous issue of parent-child relationships from the most unexpected perspective: the child's. The book dives into the minds of both the parents and the teen in hopes of extrapolating some kind of logic and reason in understanding why each behaves in the manner in which they do and why it appears quite the opposite to the other person. Van Petten not only explains what the issues are and how they come about, but how to approach them from a parental *and* teenage perspective. Unlike other experts, Van Petten highlights both sides of the story pointing out their strengths, weaknesses, and necessary improvements. The first person narration sets the tone to be friendly and light, whilst at the same time experienced and knowledgeable. The latter combines with empirical evidence from recently published medical and psychological studies to bolster the book's message and help carry it home. Van Petten confronts those issues that no one wants to talk about head on and shares a point of view that is often discarded. Well researched, well informed, and well written, *You're Grounded!* offers a truly a refreshing new look at relationships from the perspective of an educated and articulate former teenager"

—*Insight Magazine* book review
to be published when I release my book

"I read and enjoyed your book. It's a fascinating window into the lives of today's teens. I'm amazed at the maturity and balance with which you depict the roles of both teens and parents. You manage to give good advice without sounding preachy, which is a tough line to walk. If your readers can put to use any of the common sense tips you pass on, I'm sure they would benefit! You could probably market this in the global community as a "road map" to peace between nations, not just between teens and parents … As a teacher and a parent I enjoyed the glimpse into the lives of today's teens. The insights Vanessa share will help me in understanding my students and give me tools to build better communication in the classroom and at home."

—Nancy Kuechle, Middle school teacher and mother

Dedicated to:

My Mom, Anita Joy First, who has always believed in my book and helped me every step of the way. I love you.

Thank you to Dad (Vance), my other Mom (Stacy) and Pop (Larry) for your wise guidance, love and concern. Thank you to my siblings and my friends for always being there to support me. Thank you to the Illusion Factory for believing and helping me achieve my dreams. I am also very grateful to all of the people who opened up to me during their interviews—thank you for trusting me, giving me your insights and your time.

Contents

Part IV   Teenage Interaction

Introduction

"A what, Mom? A book? You want me to write a book? We had an honest, hour-long conversation about teenagers, and now you want me to write a book?"

That was it. Something as basic and honest as a conversation between mother and daughter, yet my mom thought everyone should know what we'd said.

"But that's just it," she explained. "The things you've told me are things that parents don't understand. Teachers and adults remember things differently; kids think teen life should be like what they see in the movies," my mom said.

According to my mother, one of life's mysteries and frustrations is something that I wake up to everyday—the life of a teenager.

Why do the seven years that make up a teenager's life have so many books written about them, so many doctors and specialists dealing with them, and so many magazines and TV specials focused on them? Why are the years from 13 to 19 the cause of so many psychological problems and altered life patterns?

I didn't realize how scarring and mysterious a teenager's life could be until I saw my mom's reaction to my description of what I saw in real life. Only when I concentrated and looked at everyone and everything around me, including people's reactions to teenagers and teenagers themselves, did I realize that teens and parents need a *better way* to communicate with each other. As important, teens need to identify and understand what is *really* happening around them in order to survive the teen years less scathed.

The reality is that a teenager's life is upsetting, because so much is expected of teens when they are not necessarily ready. Mistakes can cause scars that may lead to therapy bills and bad memories later on.

A teenager's life is also mysterious to adults and to teenagers themselves. For adults, the mystery lies behind the moody kids and drunken teenage parties they may pass by on a Saturday night. For us, the mystery of our own lives lies behind the very walls we set up for ourselves. These are the unspoken boundaries, rules, and patterns every single teenager lives by, whether they know it or not. It goes beyond cliques and outcasts, prom queens and jocks. Those are the stereotypes that every adult assumes is the basis of teenage problems. Popularity, parties, drugs, sex, and parents. Sure, these things can set the premises for some of the problems and adventures we can get ourselves into, but they are not what the life of a teenager is all about.

What is it all about? It is the struggle between a new set of rules and interactions in conflict with the values and beliefs your parents taught you before you turned 13 years old.

This book lies on the cusp of the truth about being a teenager today. It tells you the real story about how teens feel and think from an actual teenage perspective. It delves into what is unspoken and unacceptable in the minds of most parents and in the minds of most teenagers.

Who are teenagers, and why are they so different? Why are we so alienated from each other and our parents?

I am not writing this for the reaction. I am writing it because I have watched my friends throw their lives away, making some of the worst decisions of their lives, and I wondered why. Why, as human beings, do we treat ourselves like garbage, and do it in the same way over and over again? I am writing this book because I am watching the parents of other teenagers in my life ruin their relationships with their kids because of misunderstanding and fear. Many parents don't seem to remember (or refuse to remember) what it was like to be a teen. Perhaps no one has told you the real reasons we come home late, buy drugs, and have trouble in school.

In this book, I hope that I can tell you. I cannot speak for every teenager out there, because I am not an expert. I draw on my own experience with my parents, friends and other adults as well as information, advice and anecdotes collected from hundreds of interviews with average teenagers and parents. In this book, I have prepared, analyzed, and written the truth that I believe reflects the lives of most teens. These are the aspects of a teenager's life that we have come to fear, shun, and ignore.

For teenagers, I hope to bring to light the ignorance and blindness that we all live. We are bound up in our tight circles of studying, popularity, performance, and pressure, unable to gain any perspective from outside our narrowly focused lives. First, we have to understand who we are and what is shaping us. We need to know and identify that there are various types of teenagers, recognize the types of pressure put on us, the facades we wear, and our breaking points. I am putting on paper what is often not discussed and remains hidden. If anything, I hope that with this book teenagers can put their lives and their problems into perspective and understand that they are not alone and they have ways to change their options. I also want to give constructive advice to teenagers about how they can get along better with their parents, improve their relationships as the key to greater happiness at home, and having less groundings, fights, and misunderstandings.

For adults, I hope that this book will make you remember what you tried to forget, why you have become an adult martyr over your teenager, and enlighten you about what the life of your teenager is really like. When you understand these realities, your relationship with your teenager should improve, because you will know where they are coming from, and you will be able to communicate with them better.

This book is divided into four parts. Part I, "The Basics," provides an overview of contemporary scientific research on teenagers and parents to shed light on the chemical explanations for common behaviors and disagreements. Also in this section, teenagers and parents can honestly evaluate their own relationship and what needs to be changed.

Part II, "The Teenage Pressure Cooker," is a look into the life and various stressors of an average teenager. I end with suggestions and advice on how parents can help their teenagers deal with this pressure as well as tricks and coping methods for teens to successfully make it through the teenage years.

Part III, "What Parents Fear," delves into how drugs, sex, racism, driving and the Internet affect the lives of teenagers. I provide tips for dealing with 'the sex talk,' driving rules, Internet freedoms and alternative safe activities.

Part IV, "The Teenage Interaction," addresses common issues arising with cliques, bullies and dating. By discussing difficult aspects of high school social interactions, teenagers can feel less alienated and parents more included.

For all of you computer-savvy readers, this book is available as an Ebook on our website: www.YoureGroundedBook.com.

Background

Many of the problems that adults deal with stem from what happened to them in their teenage years and in childhood. Issues relating to friends, motivation, self-esteem, careers, and relationships became embedded in their psyche as children and teens and were carried into adulthood, often with no recognition or analysis of the issues. Many adults, therefore, share the same issues with their teenage children, but the adult is dealing with them in a biologically older body. Of course, many adults do recognize and work through issues from younger years. Whether or not the issues are the same or different between parent and teen, creating an opening and space to share perspectives and talk about differences can allow a teenager to feel understood and valued. This will permit the teen to relate better to the parent and even feel safer during the turbulent teenage years. If by reading this book adults and teenagers are able to see their differences and commonalities and work out their individual problems, we might be able to lessen the negative and isolating aspects of teenage life. To have stronger communication with each other as teenagers and with our parents can ameliorate the pressures of the teenage years and provide the opportunity for us to become happier and healthier adults.

You might be wondering how this book can help you bridge this gap. I will talk about the chemical and emotional aspects of being a teenager in an attempt to give adults a better understanding of the teenagers in their lives. That understanding is the first step towards a better connection and better communication. Teenagers will be also able to understand the differences between themselves and the adults in their lives. Perhaps with that information, there will be a lessening of the confusion and frustration teenagers feel when dealing with "stubborn" adults.

I have interviewed more than 750 adults, teenagers, and parents about their relationships with each other. I have seen how teenagers interact both from my own experiences and by the way the media portrays us. While the interviews were often informal and were not intended to be part of a scientific or academic study, the content of the interviews are nonetheless valuable. As a teenager grappling with my own teen parent tug of war, interviewees, especially teen participants felt comfortable telling me their honest opinions. Another advantage of the informal setting was my ability to ask questions beyond what a strictly scientific survey would allow. For example the most helpful and enlightening answers I received were in response to the question: "What would you like to tell, ask or advise your parent or teenager, but feel too embarrassed or uncomfortable to ask?"

My interviews were conducted in many different settings, such as carpools, after class teacher interviews, focus groups and even casual conversations with friends' parents. This enabled me to talk to people of all ages, religions, races and backgrounds.

Many of the adults I talked to were asked, "What do you think is different about being a teenager today versus being a teenager at the time when you were teenagers?"

The answers varied tremendously. Some of the adults thought that being a teenager today was exactly the same as it was when they were teens, while others thought that it must be completely different but weren't quite sure how. Every single one of the parents I interviewed, however, speculated about the differences. I was encouraged to think that parents <u>wanted</u> to understand us and were trying to determine what they needed to know to "get it".

I know for a fact that every teenager, no matter what the time period, has many of the same core issues. By talking to so many different adults and teens, I was able to see simple patterns that hinder the teenage-parent relationship. Issues that span the generations include self-esteem, cliques, popularity, and the opposite sex. Other factors in a teenager's life vary depending on surroundings and time period. These include racism, media, homosexuality, and political climate.

This book is based on the premise that there is no one type of teenager. We cannot be generalized into one group. We are individual people, unique and distinct, even though we may share certain issues.

About the Author

I have tried to leave my own background and personal situation out of the major themes of the book. Yet, many of my own beliefs and experiences have shaped the opinions I have. I believe my life is fairly comparable to that of most teenagers.

My parents divorced when I was four years old. I believe it was the best thing that ever happened to me. My parents each remarried and I grew up in two different households, with two different dynamics, and two different religions. In one, I grew up as the only child with my Mom and stepdad, who I called Pop, and in the other with my Dad and my stepmom, who I also called Mom, and three siblings—Robert. Courtney and Haley. I am a native Los Angelina, but have traveled inside the US and to the UK, France, Switzerland, Australia, Spain and China, on leadership and cultural programs, where I met and learned from other teenagers with different backgrounds.

I went to a public coed elementary school and attended an all-girls High School in Los Angeles named Marlborough School for Girls. I believe my all-girls education has helped shape me into a better person and has given me the foundation to write this book. I attended Emory University in Atlanta and received my BA in Chinese and International Politics. I am fluent in Spanish, Chinese, and English, and I have a working knowledge of French. I hope to work with international businesses in China.

My Research for This Book

I have been very fortunate to study abroad and in political and leadership programs in the United States. As a result I have met many different teenagers of all ages, from all backgrounds and socioeconomic levels, going to different schools and coming from all over the world. When I decided to write this book, I talked to my friends from all over and their parents, resulting in over 750 interviews. I combine these interviews, my own experiences with my parents, the media, and my overall research. I have babysat for many different families and worked as a camp counselor and leader of a youth group. Through all of these activities I observed teenagers in different family and social settings and deduced various patterns between teenagers and their parents. I integrated them with my own reflections and experiences of life as a teenager in today's world.

PART I
The Basics

Groundbreaking Science and the Teenage Brain

"I feel like I am sometimes on a different planet than my parents, the music they listen to, the food they like. How could they have ever been teenagers before?"
  -Teenager, 17

PBS' Frontline interviewed Yurgelun-Todd, the director of neurophysiology and cognitive neuroimaging at McLean Hospital in Belmont, Massachusetts. The research she did about the differences between a teenager's brain and an adult's brain provides explanations for the differences in behavior between adults and teenagers.

Frontline's "Inside the Teenage Brain"
www.pbs.org/wgbh/pages/frontline/shows/teenbrain/ect/aliens.html

Todd examined teenage and adult brains through an MRI as they responded to a series of pictures. The volunteers were told to discern the kind of emotion that was displayed. Todd and her researchers discovered that the teenagers and adults were using two completely different parts of the brain in interpreting the facial expressions, even though the series of pictures shown to each group was identical.
The frontal part of the brain is the area that plans, acts out, anticipates outcomes, and/or sets goals. This part of the brain also makes executive decisions and carries out judgment through thought processes. The adults in the study used this part of the brain when discerning the emotion of the faces in the pictures.
Teenagers, unlike adults, used "the more inferior or lower part of the brain which has been associated with emotion and gut responses." This part of the brain was more activated in the teenager when determining the emotions on the faces as compared to the adults who used more of the frontal lobe and/or a combination of the two areas.

These huge differences in brain patterns help explain the differences between adult and teenage behavior. The teenager often responds to situations with more of a gut or emotional response while adults often think things through and use more judgment. In the study by Todd, 100 percent of the adults identified the emotion of the picture correctly while only <u>50 percent</u> of the teenagers correctly identified the emotion!

This research helps us to understand why teenagers tend to act more impulsively and take more risks. Unlike adults, they are not weighing their options or thinking about consequences. What a relief for a parent to know that their teenager may literally be unable to comply easily with a parent's wishes, because the teen's brain is responding from a different place, using different rules. The teen may not want to be difficult or unpredictable, but he or she has brain functions dictating a response. If a teen knows that he or she thinks differently from their parent because biological age is dictating a response resulting in an unacceptable outcome, a teen can stop and look at the situation from a different perspective. Indeed, this difference in brain structure illuminates why parents and teenagers often think they do not understand each other.

"One of the interesting things about the findings is that they suggest that the teenagers are not able to correctly read all of the feelings in the adult face. So that would suggest to us that when they're relating to their parents or to their friends' parents or to their teachers, they may be misperceiving or misunderstanding some of the feelings that we have as adults … if you're assuming they understand everything you said—they may not have. Or they may have understood it differently. And if you think that their assignments are clear to them, they may not be. So it may be that we're putting them in a difficult situation because we're assuming that our conversation is very clear when, in fact, they may also think they've understood it clearly; but we're not saying the same things to each other."

I found this study groundbreaking and incredibly helpful in dealing with my parents. I realized that the reason we argue or sometimes misunderstand each other is actually *physiological.* Instead of feeling frustrated and lost and saying, "My parents just don't understand me," I actually knew it was true. The same goes for parents. If parents realize that some of their teenager's irrational or impulsive decisions are physiological and based on brain function, the parents might be less frustrated and more patient. In return, their understanding could stimulate more cooperation from the teen.

Frontline gives a great example.

"A typical Saturday morning conversation where there are a number of small things that a child or adolescent would be told to do. 'Put your dish in the sink. Please get dressed now. We're going to get ready to go out.' And ten minutes later, there seems to be no movement; the dish is not in the sink and they're not dressed. And the first response as an adult is that the child or adolescent is being difficult or confrontational or not wanting to do it.

But in fact, a lot of the time, they're just not paying attention; either they heard that information, but they didn't really register it, or they heard it and they thought it was OK to do it later. Or they heard it, but whatever came on TV seemed more important. They somehow have reorganized that information, so they're not really trying to disappoint you or frustrate you. It's just that they saw it in a different light...."

Here are some interesting facts to help teens and parents communicate better.

- Ninety-five percent of the human brain is developed by the age of six.

- Different responses to emotional stimulation develop between the ages of 11 years and 17 years, with the biggest differences occurring in the early teen years.

- School is important! According to studies, the brain is much more responsive earlier in life than it is later in life to "enrichment or special kinds of education." More stimulation means a smarter and more adaptable brain.

Another aspect explored by Dr. Todd and her researchers was the difference between the female and male teenage brain. The study showed females were more accurate than the males in guessing the facial emotions correctly. Females were "also a little bit more subdued, relative to males.... In general, the males in our studies showed more reaction from that gut region of the brain, and less frontal or executive reaction." These findings offer another scientific explanation concerning why boys are usually bigger risk takers than girls.

Next time there is an argument, disagreement, or misunderstood order in your household, remember the scientific differences between the teenage and adult brains. It is not only reassuring, but it is also enlightening and can be the basis for discussion instead of confrontation.

Menopause and Adolescence

"Sometimes I yell and I have no idea why I am yelling, and sometimes I yell because no one is listening to me from the last time I exploded."
    -Mother, 53, who claims to be in the midst of menopause

"I think estrogen makes my mom psycho."
    -Male teenager, 15, about his theory about how menopause affects his mom

You have already heard some scientific reasons why parents and teenagers can disagree and misunderstand each other. Another reason that may not be so obvious to parents, teens, and adults has to do with what some mothers are going through emotionally and hormonally.

Doctors, best friends, and magazines give hormones as the reason for the angst and disgruntled moody feelings in a teenager's life and demeanor. Factually, teenagers' hormones are raging as they course through us in ways we have never before experienced. Those hormones influence our thoughts, behaviors, and attitudes. But, who ever thinks about what is going on for some mothers hormonally?

As I sat and listened to some of my friends complain bitterly about the fights they were having with their mothers about the laundry or weekend plans, I couldn't help but think that the excessive amount of emotion that typically strains the mother-teenage relationship may be based not only on our hormones or having a bad day. There had to be something else. I came home and started to research the physical and emotional effects and reactions of hormones on teenagers. It was then that I realized that menopausal women suffer from the same effects!

Many women reach menopause from ages 45 to 55. Many teenagers have mothers between the ages of 45 to 55. This is especially true as women have entered the workforce and opted to defer having children while establishing their careers. The number of older mothers has reached record numbers and is growing. Deferring childbearing has the effect of having menopausal mothers who are rearing teens during what will be a hormonally challenging time for mother <u>and</u>

child. Add midlife for a husband/father who is in his 40s or 50s as he faces a teen with new needs, and you have a recipe for family disaster, unless everyone educates themselves on the issues and gains some coping strategies.

If teenagers go through puberty at the same time that their mothers go through menopause, there is likely to be house chaos and war. Let's look at some of the symptoms that teenagers and menopausal women share.[1]

Teenagers:		Menopausal Women:	
Physical:	**Emotional:**	**Physical:**	**Emotional:**
Weight gain	Depression	Weight gain	Depression
Breast discomfort	Anxiety	Breast tenderness	Anxiety
Increased appetite	Irritability	Increased appetite	Irritability
Muscle/joint pain	Loss of motivation	Muscle/joint pain	Loss of Motivation

Of course, the list goes on. For menopausal women, these symptoms include hot flashes, dizziness, memory loss, and nervous tension. For teenagers, the symptoms include increased body awareness, growing pains, and increased sexual appetite at top the list.

As you can see, some life experiences and emotional challenges are the same for teenagers and for women going through menopause. Knowing this makes it easier to understand why mothers and their teenagers can have huge emotional blowouts and misunderstandings—**they both have mood swings, depression and irritability! No wonder there is so much fighting going on!**

The misunderstandings between teenagers and their fathers can be hormonally based as well. Fathers lose testosterone as they age. They recognize that certain dreams and goals may not be achieved. Prostate issues may cause sexual dysfunction and a feeling of being less than a man. Many men experience these issues but have no skill set for recognizing their feelings and putting them into words. Their resulting confusion and upset state makes life very difficult to handle. Add to this mix a hysterical teen and a wife going through the change, and it is a wonder that teens survive to adulthood.

---

1.   July 18, 2006. <http://www.medicinenet.com/menopause/article.htm.>

Teen/Parent Perceptions

In my interviews with parents and teenagers, I asked volunteers many questions, some of which are listed below:

To teens:

1.   What are some stereotypes you have about adults?

2.   What are some of the stereotypes you think adults have about teenagers?

3.   Do you think they are true?

4.   Do you respect your parents or other adults?

To adults:

1.   What are some of the stereotypes you have about teenagers?

2.   What are some of the stereotypes you think teenagers have about adults?

3.   Do you think they are true?

4.   Do you respect teenagers?

These questions were meant to establish some of the major trends in the teenage/adult points of view to help teenagers and adults understand each other. For adults, knowing what teenagers think about them can help to motivate adults to reconsider their attitudes and beliefs. For teenagers, it is important to understand that a significant aspect of the common level of disrespect many adults hold toward teens is based on stereotypes and often untrue perceptions about teens. Teens can help if they know the nature of the misconceptions projected upon them.

Teenage Responses

1. What are some stereotypes you have about adults?

    "They think that whatever they say is right."

    "They think all teenagers are crazy."

    "They are strict and stubborn."

    "They never admit they are wrong."

    "They are disconnected, set in their own ways, and always think it is the teenager who has to change."

    "They don't know how to have fun."

2. What are some of the stereotypes that you think adults have about teenagers?

    "We are crazy and horribly behaved animals."

    "We are rowdy troublemakers."

    "We cause problems and make too much noise."

    "They think we are all on drugs."

    "They think that we don't think."

3. Do you think these stereotypes are true?

    "Hell, no."

    "The fact that they think that, makes us want to live up to their expectations."

    "We aren't crazy—it is called hormones!"

    "We aren't as bad as they think."

    "Sometimes we can party, but we are not all or always like that."

4. Do you respect your parents or other adults?

    "Sometimes."

    "Yeah, I really think I respect them a lot more than they respect us."

"Usually."

"No, not really, but I pretend like I do."

"Of course … I am a little angel."

Adult Responses

1. What are some of the stereotypes you have about teenagers?

    "They are very experimental and open-minded."

    "There are a lot of rebellion issues, and usually curiosity gets in their way."

    "Emotionally unstable and erratic."

    "Very concerned with peer pressure and appearances."

    "They think that their friendships with other peers are more important than their relationships with their parents."

    "The males are really disrespectful."

    "Vivacious, but with some definite depression issues."

2. What are some of the stereotypes that you think teenagers have about adults?

    "That we are straight-laced and conservative."

    "Foreign, set in their ways, and totally different than teenagers."

    "Unapproachable and that we think we are better than the teenagers."

    "Boring and no fun."

    "Authorities with no clue of what is hip and what teenagers need."

3. Do you think they are true?

    "Oh, no, parents are usually just being so repressive because of fear."

    "We were all teenagers once, and we all thought the same things about adults."

    "Maybe the strictness that adults have is because we are trying to protect our teenagers."

    "No, we are all teenagers at heart."

4. Do you respect teenagers?

    "I respect teenagers, but I think that they should respect adults even more."

    "I do respect teenagers."

    "I respect teenagers as long as they respect me."

There is a commonality in these responses. Adults think teenagers are wild, and teenagers actually know that this is how adults perceive them. Teenagers essentially think that adults are strict and close-minded, and adults actually know that this is how teens perceive them. Both teenagers and parents are aware of these perceptions, but find them **false.** Teens <u>disagreed</u> with the perception that they are generally wild and untrustworthy, and adults <u>disagreed</u> with the perception that they don't listen and are too strict. So, how can teens and adults adjust their behavior not only to change the perceptions each has of the other, but also to improve the quality and nature of their interactions?

There are specific things teenagers can do to improve relationships with adults as well as specific actions that adults can take to improve their relationships with their teens. In order to begin that process, teens and their parents must <u>get to know each other</u>. I know that sounds strange. They lived together for 14 plus years, and now they must get acquainted? The answer is a categorical yes. The young man or young woman living in your house, parents, is <u>not</u> the same person you have been dressing, feeding, and caring for since birth. The passage of time, the pressures of young adulthood, the influence of peers, and raging hormones have shaped this child into someone you may not recognize. It's time to reconnect. Teens may be resistant. That's normal. They are trying to individualize and find their own way. Be patient, and know that it is not a one-way process. Teens need to allow their parents access to their lives and open up, as hard as that can be, to the new personality and inner thoughts that are brewing. The following chapters provide some possible questions to help open the dialogue for the new relationship waiting to be embraced.

How Well Do You Know Each Other?

"My Dad thinks Green Day is like Earth day, but I tell him no, it's my favorite band."

-Teenager, 14

"I think my daughter thinks we play scrabble when we go out, but we are not that old."

-A mother commenting about what her daughter thinks she does with her free time.

If you and your teen are willing, the best way to achieve a better and more communicative, trusting relationship is for each of you to read this book so you can get on the same page. Here is a questionnaire to see how well you really know each other. Parents should answer the questions for parents <u>as well as</u> read the questions being posed to teens to see if they can anticipate the answers. Teens should do the same, i.e., answer their questions and read and think about the answers their parents might give to the adult's questions. At the end of the questionnaire, teens should read the answers to their parent aloud and vice versa. How closely did each of you anticipate the other's answers?

Parent Questionnaire about Your Teen.

The facts:

1) What is your teen's favorite band or music artist?

2) What is your teen's favorite food?

3) Does your teenager have a best friend? What is his or her name?

4) Where does your teenager usually hang out on the weekends?

5) What is your teenager's favorite subject in school?

6) Who is your teenager's least favorite teacher? Name?

Little deeper:

7) If your teenager could change one thing about himself or herself what would it be?

8) What takes up the most time in your teenager's life?

9) What irritates your teen the most on a daily basis?

10) What is your teen's most serious problem or issue in his or her life right now?

11) Who are your teen's heroes?

12) Does your teenager trust you?

13) Would your teenager feel comfortable coming to you with a serious problem?

Teen Questionnaire about Your Parent

The facts:

1) What is your mom's maiden name?

2) What are your parents' favorite colors?

3) What do your parents do during their free time?

4) What are your parents' favorite movies?

5) Where did your parents go to High School?

6) What are your parents' favorite musical artists?

7) What do your parents actually do for a living? If they go to work, what do they actually do in their jobs?

Little Deeper:

8) What is the biggest issue in your parents' life right now?

9) What do your parents want for you?

10) What do you think irritates your parents most on a daily basis?

11) What takes up the most time in your parents' lives?

12) Do your parents trust you?

13) What are some of your parents' strongest morals or beliefs—the ones they live by?

PART II
The Teenage PressureCooker

College. Grades. Friends. Cliques. Parents. Image. What is it that makes these things so daunting?

Many people question a teenager's reasons for being stressed. They question the justification behind our complaining, our depressions, and our moods. The point of this chapter is to allow parents and adults to see and understand the pressures we face. I hope by looking at the types of pressures and situations to which teenagers are subjected, parents and teens can figure out solutions. These solutions will certainly lessen the stress of a teenager's/parent's life and, as a result, alleviate some of the pressure and tension that exists in the adult/teen relationship.

I also hope that as teenagers read about some of the stress factors they all experience, they will feel less alone. It is important to realize that other young adults are suffering from similar issues.

Adults often use hormones as the primary reason for teenage angst. It is easier for adults to assume teens have less pressure in their lives than to acknowledge the fact that they themselves might be a reason for our stress. Why is it that the highest incidence of suicide is among people between the ages of 16 and 24?[1] Why is it that teens are almost always blamed for being the rowdiest and most insecure people in our society?

According to Dr. Charles Wibbelsman, a teenager's greatest worry and source of stress is relayed in one single question: "Am I normal?"[2]

Now, mind you, I personally have neither asked my magic Eight Ball that question, nor have I ever deemed myself abnormal, overly normal, or perfectly normal. Instead, in this section I summarized and categorized a teenager's pressures, internal and external, according to my survey of teenagers and my own personal experience. I hope that these ideas will enlighten parents and adults about what teenagers really worry about.

1. National Institute of Mental Health. In Harm's Way: Suicide in America. Accessed January 24, 2005 <http://nimh.nih.gov/publicat/harmsway.cfm>

2. Wibbelsman, Charles. "A Teenager's Greatest Worry." The Parenting Resource Center on the Web. Oct. 24, 1995. <http://www.parentsplace.com/>

Sources of Pressure

"How could she be stressed, she has no bills, no job, and no teenagers!"

-Mother, 48, on her dermatologists comment that her daughter's acne came from stress

College and Our Futures

As I sat down in the information meeting run by a college admissions officer for a prestigious Ivy League school, I got out my notepad and pen so I could take notes. This year I would be visiting 37 different college campuses, attending 28 information sessions on various schools, and meeting with admissions officers from deans of colleges who would be visiting at my school in Los Angeles. All that would mean a lot of walking, a lot of college stats, and a lot of pressure.

I was doing fine at this particular point in my first college tour. I ended up going on three tours that covered the East and West Coast colleges. I saw part of the campuses, and as I walked on them, I felt they definitely lived up to their reputation and my own standards. The standards I used consisted of things my friends and family had told me as well as what I had heard about these schools in movies.

At Princeton, as the formidable Admissions Director began his speech, I thought, _Cool. I could see myself here. I just have to get in._

"Good morning, and welcome to Princeton. Let's be honest here. Almost every single person in this room will apply here, and probably none of you will get in."

Huh?! I thought to myself. _Well, it is good to know I won't get in, considering I just flew across the country to visit this school._

He continued to talk about the school's amazing programs and campus, and I couldn't help but wonder why he was wasting his breath on a group from whom he believed no students would be admitted. Keep in mind this man had not met any of the people in our group, and for all he knew, he could have been disparaging a group of Junior Olympic athletes with perfect 1600 SAT scores and 4.5 grade point averages.

What a disappointing afternoon for all of us to be addressed in such a demeaning manner.

College is huge. We are reminded of this fact continuously throughout high school. To us it sounds like, "Out of all of the decisions you will make in your life, where you go to college is one of the biggest. If you do not put your mind toward getting into a superior college, it will negatively impact your life." We hear it from our parents, our teachers, our college counselors, our friends, and worst of all from our own minds. We see it in our own dreams, and we know that it is the first major decision we will ever have to make, and supposedly, one of the most important.

College and our not-so-immediate future are constant sources of pressure for teenagers. Competition is incredibly tough today. College applicants have better grades, higher test scores, and cooler extracurricular activities than ever. If the rush to get into the best-known, top tier universities is a foot race, the track is now clogged with four-minute milers. (Mathews)[1]

To even be considered by top universities, we have to be good in *everything*. That means that we not only have to get good grades and have good test scores, we also have to be good athletes or artists, do community service, and have great essays, recommendations, and leadership experiences.

More teenagers than ever before are going to college, and as a result more teenagers are stressed from the process. With the number of applications so high, competition is fiercer than ever, making the process itself more stressful. More qualified people are applying. Students know college degrees are now required for many good jobs. However, getting into college is not the only worry. Once students make it through the application process, they have to excel in college in order to get into good graduate schools. Then, of course, they have to find steady jobs which allow them to earn enough money to support themselves and their families in a society where unemployment grows by the day.

Some Facts

It is true not everyone goes to college. In fact, only about 20% of all high school students in America end up going to college. About 60% to 67% of high school graduates who matriculate at a college or university actually end up completing college, up from 49% in 1972. Today, 37% of university students had parents who never went to college.*

---

1.   Mathews, Jay. "How to Get into Every College on your List." Washington Post Company, Aug. 17, 2004.

The 2001 survey done by the Institute of Higher Education states that the number one reason students go to college is to get a better job than would be possible with only a high school diploma. A close second is the desire to gain a "general education and appreciation of ideas", followed by the ability to make more money with a college degree.

The survey represents approximately 1.2 million entering freshmen at more than 421 four-year universities nationwide. The 2001 survey suggests America's students are more serious about a higher education than many adults would believe.

Adults too often assume that teenagers do not care about their future and their schooling. Teenagers are known to roll their eyes and moan at even the slightest mention of weekend homework, getting a head start on college applications, or working ahead into next week's homework. The government's assiduous efforts to keep kids in school, lower the high school dropout rate, and increase school attendance are ever growing.

But these apparent signs of rebellion and disinterest **are not necessarily indicative of a teenager's laziness**. Rather, they may mirror the reality that teenagers fear disappointment, whether it is from friends, parents, or themselves. They may elect not to put themselves out there to try wholeheartedly because they may fail, and if they do, they can console themselves with the excuse that they really didn't try anyway.

Teenagers also act on their natural instinct. The instinct to be independent and to make our own decisions is strong. The rebellions, comebacks, and fights are often reactions to the fear and pressure that we feel and are also the results of not wanting to be told what to do or how to do it.

By relieving pressure and dealing with common teenage stressors more effectively, adult and teenage relationships will improve along with teenage productivity.

Next I will explore why teenagers are so fearful and why they rebel. I will also outline some tricks to help relieve some of the tension.

School

Period 1: "Final exam Monday morning on the background of Newton and his theories. Study, study, study."

Period 2: "Do not forget to do the essay over the weekend, and remember, it is half of your grade this semester."

Period 3: "I want the reading of chapters 33 through 37 done with extensive outline notes; be prepared to answer questions in class on Monday."

Period 4: "Finish all of the problems on the handout and the worksheet, and for goodness sakes, commit those formulas to memory; we have things to do."

Period 5: "Quiz Monday morning. Prepare your terms."

"Uh ... Mrs. Smith, we have a lot of homework already assigned this weekend. Do you think it would be ok if you postponed the quiz until Tuesday?"

"What, is my class not as important to you? You will prepare for the quiz on Monday, and if you tell me you cannot take it then, you will get a zero for this assessment. Have a good weekend."

There are two ways a teenager can react to this school pressure. The first (and most traveled route) is to ignore all of the homework and take the bad grades and the punishments later in class, which makes you see how the downward, "I don't care about school" spiral gets started. The second is to plow through the work, try to stay in a good mood over the weekend, and get some social time squeezed in between finishing your homework and family time/parent talking time/chores that must be done. Sometimes, if your child seems distant, it is really because they have a lot of work and then <u>need</u> to have social time. If your parents want you to have family dinner with them, and are insistent upon your staying home on a Saturday night instead of going out, it is probably because they don't realize what is going on for you in your life.

For a teenager, the best way to shorten the required amount of family time is go <u>against</u> your initial instinct not to tell your parents anything that is going on in your life. If you have a big project, **tell them about it**. If you need some space with your friends because of a particularly busy week in school and sports practice, tell them why. Parents are more inclined to let you do things if they know what is going on with you. And keep in mind, you are underage, and they do have a *right* to know what you are doing. Talking to your parents and letting them know what is going on in your life is important and can help you as well as them.

The benefits of talking to your parents include these positive outcomes:

1. Having someone else with whom to share your worries. Despite what you may think, your parents have gone through a lot and might have some really good advice for you.

2. It will make your relationship with your parents better and allow them to understand you and your schedule so you get in less fights with each other, and then, in turn, have more freedom.

3. Encourage your parents to be empathetic and more flexible with you when they understand the pressure you are under.

No matter how enigmatic the teenage generation and their problems may be, everyone remembers how stressful school is. Between Advanced Placement tests, SATs, and just regular homework, teenagers today have more expected of them than any other generation. Most Advanced Placement Courses require 1-2 hours of homework per night with other courses requiring 30 minutes to one hour per night as well. So, if a student is only taking regular courses, which is not encouraged for those students looking to go to university, that student would be doing an average of four hours of homework per night. And we wonder why all teenagers cannot just pop out those A's. That's a lot of homework, no matter what your perspective is on any other matter related to teenagers.

Add to homework pressure the issues of cliques, the opposite sex, and other social dilemmas, and school becomes a literal pressure cooker. The current high school curriculum places students in a three-tiered balancing act. Students are expected to be able to finish homework from seven classes, many of which are already at college level, participate in extra-curricular activities in school such as sports and clubs, and maintain a decent grade point average by studying for numerous tests and quizzes that may all fall on the same day.

Many adults don't realize that some high schools are now as hard or harder than most colleges. You would never take seven college courses all in the same semester at university and be expected to do well in them all. Yet, this is what is required and expected of many high school students. Why? Because in order to get into a good college or university, students are packed with the maximum and hardest course load offered because it beefs up your transcript.

One of my close friends ran into this exact "transcript" problem. As an extremely conscientious and diligent student with straight A's, she always took the hardest classes to constantly challenge herself and strengthen her transcript. All through high school she wanted to take a psychology course offered at my school. As a senior, she worked her schedule around to finally include the course. To work the class in, she was forced to drop a "solid" subject, i.e., a math, science, English, history or language course. This left her with *only* Advanced Placement physics, Calculus accelerated, Advanced Placement Government, and Advanced Placement English. Her college counselor and the dean of students told her that if she dropped her history class to take a psychology class, she would only have four solids, and this would not look impressive to colleges. She came out of their offices crying. She had always wanted to take psychology and now, after four years, when she could finally do it, the adults at our school told her she wasn't working hard enough, despite the fact she was in four AP classes! She ended up taking psychology and adding an AP course in a language in which she was already fluent, simply to beef up her transcript.

This kind of constant pressure at school sends the message, "Your effort is never enough, <u>you</u> are never enough."

More on the Two Reactions

There are two ways that teenagers react to the pressures of school, homework, and college admissions. The first is to take all of the hard classes and continue to study endlessly until the teen is completely burned out and frustrated. The school's pressure ruins the high school experience and discourages the once-determined students from continuing with schooling. Meanwhile, the constant studying, overblown class schedules, excessive busy-work homework assignments, and an incessant focus on college admission makes teenage students sick and irritable. This becomes the fundamental source of a great deal of tension between parents and their kids.

Because students are so burned out when it comes time for summer, all they want to do is sit around, watch TV and sleep in. Of course, parents want their kids to get summer jobs, go to camp, do community service, etc.

How many times at the beginning of summer do you hear or say, "Get up off the couch and <u>do</u> something! I will not have you sitting around all summer!"

Well, now we can understand why kids want to get home on the weekends or during summer and just sit. It is because school pressures and homework burn us out.

Maybe students make it through high school working extremely hard, getting summer jobs, and getting into a great school. These students get to university and realize that they are completely burned out. Let me tell you, this is the wrong place to feel burned out! On my freshman hall alone, three students had breakdowns within the first semester of college and had to take a break and go home. They never had a break because high school was so demanding!

Alternatively, your child may be burned out from never resting during high school. When he gets to college, he will have the attitude, "Screw work. I just got out of working so hard to get in here." Then they binge drink, use drugs, and go to parties. I know many people who went to college and either had to take a mid-semester break at home, or partied so hard in fraternities and sororities their grades plummeted. Please realize this and find the balance between work and play earlier.

This is a warning to parents. If you do not help your kids find a good balance between homework, going out, and family time early in their teenage years, your kids will find it by experimenting themselves.

This leads to rebellion.

The second reaction a teenager may have is to ignore the requirements and demands and rebel against all of the required work. Their rebellion, fear, and avoidance of the pressure manifest themselves in drugs, sex, and violence. Teenagers become so overwhelmed with the demands of their school and the expectations of their parents that they completely tune them out. They start breaking rules, staying out late, skipping class, and taking drugs to escape from the pressure and demands of school. Of course, this is the extreme reaction. Many students go through waves of feeling so overwhelmed they tune out and sleep all the time, or waves where school is not so bad. Wherever you or your child lies, it is important to realize the feeling overwhelmed of stressed is normal and the best way to alleviate the pressure is to find some alternative outlets.

We end up working hard in high school simply to get into a good college. We get into a good college so that we can get a good job to then get a better job. We look forward to a life of long, hard hours at the job of our choice—except most times you don't get the ideal job. Why? All so that in the last twenty years of your life you can live with a basic level of comfort. Teenagers do need to work for future goals, but the pressures in our lives take us out of the moment and keep us from enjoying our lives as they are.

Friends and Social Status

Dear Diary,

I think Sarah is really mad at me. Today I walked by her in the hallway, and not only did she not say hi, but she also gave me this look. I know she is mad at me. It was the way she looked at me. What am I going to do? I am not sure what I did, but it was probably bad if she is that angry at me....
-Female, 17

Dear Me,

I want this year to be a totally new year! I am going to get in with the popular crowd and be friends with all of the cheerleaders. I have to make sure I get rid of all of my bad qualities. I can't laugh too loud or talk about stupid movies. I have to start listening to the cool music stations and memorize all of the words, even to the songs I don't really like. They have to like me. I have to be popular this year....
-Female, 15, making a list of her new school year resolutions

Dear Journal,

There is this party this weekend all of my friends are going to. It is at Nick's house, and I don't like him, but I have to go. I mean, all of the girls will be there, and I am going to have to look really good in front of my friends so Chelsea will like me....
-Male, 17, debating whether or not to go to the party on Friday night

Dear Diary,

I hate my English class. Jessica and her group are in the class, and I swear they snicker at me when I make comments. I have to be sure to stay quiet in class the rest of the week so they don't laugh at me. Maybe Molly will invite me over to tan by her pool.
-Female, 16, upset over the mean girls in her English class

Dear Journal,

... I have to start smoking **so they will hang out with me** ...

Dear Diary,

... What if they **don't like me** ...

Dear Journal,

... I have to be **what they want me to be** ...

Dear Diary,

... I wish I were in the **cool group** ...

Dear Journal,

... I try to be funny but sometimes they just **laugh and make fun of me** ...

Dear Diary,

... I caught all of my friends **talking behind my back** ...

Whether written in a diary, or thought about in class, or told to a best friend or sibling, these are some of the thoughts that float through a typical teenager's mind everyday. How is it that with school and our futures looming over our heads, we even have the time to think about friends? And why should friends be such a big stressor anyway? The answer is because friends make up most of a teenager's life. They are in school, they are in college, they can be at home, in your extracurricular activities, while giving you input on everything from your clothes to what classes you should and should not take. Just as the laws of nature occupy animals in the wild, the brutal underlying rules of the teen kingdom are some of the largest pressures on our minds—rules which are followed both consciously and unconsciously.

It was the look, the way he said it, the flouting. It is these underlying interactions that define the way teenagers interact with each other. Social status and friends are different from the pressures of school and college in that we can sometimes escape schoolwork or parental/family pressure. With school we get a break during summer, and the real college pressure doesn't start until the second year of high school. But friends and popularity are always issues. School is not only filled with work and expectations, it is also a place where teens are expected to see and be seen, unmasked and stripped down to all of the things that we really are.

In the "Types of Teenagers and Teenage Interaction" section, I take a closer look at the world of popularity and classification among teenagers. I also challenge and define the Rules of Teenage Interactions that have been described to me by other teenagers. Yet, the social pressures of being popular are a constant source of stress for teenagers. As seen in the examples above, the social pressures consist of everything from what group you are in, to other people's opinions of you, to what party you are going to, to what you are going to do when you get there.

Our Body Image and the Way We Look

Body image is another way that teenagers instigate internal pressure. The social pressures of looking good are triggered by the media, magazines, and, of course, the teenagers themselves. Having a nice body and wearing the hippest clothes contribute to a constant struggle to impress and gain approval from the opposite sex and friends.

An image that pops into your head when you think about teen body image is often a girl in her mid-teens who throws up after she eats a big meal, counts her calories, and/or constantly compares herself to supermodels and actresses. We do not think about the issue of boys who are driven to bulimia, anorexia, and compulsive exercising. What else besides the media drives teenagers to hate their bodies and abuse them?

Parents

When I was seven years old, I remember standing in the supermarket line with my best friend and her mom, while she read a tabloid. There was an article about obesity in kids. Her mom started reading it and bent back the paper pages to show us the pictures of kids who "were going to eat themselves to death," her mother said. As I stood there perplexed about not only the word obesity, but also about how someone could eat themselves to death, hre mother promptly shut the magazine and put it back on the shelf.

Her mother, of course, did not want to plant a seed of body image awareness in our heads. Then again does any parent *want* to have their kids take anything negative so seriously? Her mother doesn't even remember this. Yet, from that moment in the supermarket on, I became increasingly aware of how much I was eating, and I worried that I would eat myself to death. I started to notice that my parents constantly dieted and that my dad was always going to the doctor for thyroid problems, saying that if he got it fixed, he would finally be able to lose some weight.

When I was 11 years old, I started to horde chips and candy bars in my bedroom. I would save up my allowance and buy candy with it. I'd hide the chips in my room under my bed, anywhere really. Not because I wasn't being fed, but because I didn't want my parents to see that I was eating myself to death. At that point in my life I was a chubby little kid with a short haircut and braces. My parents wanted me to lose weight, so I hid the food they didn't want me to eat and feared I was going to die of obesity. Mind you, I was not even close to being obese. I simply had a case of some extra baby fat.

My parents finally found all of my stashed food and decided to send me to a nutritionist when I was 12 years old. Before going to the nutritionist, I finally learned what obesity was, and I realized that I was not going to eat myself to death. I also knew I had to lose weight. I understood only recently that my parents sent me to the nutritionist so I could understand what healthy eating was. My normal diet consisted mainly of hamburgers, macaroni and cheese, hotdogs and beans, pizza, an occasional "tater tot" and many fruit roll-ups. While my parents wanted me to learn what healthy eating was, I went on the nutritionist's program to lose weight.

I began weighing my food on little scales, recording every piece of food put in my mouth, and dreading the one day a week I had to get weighed at the nutritionist's office. I did end up losing 30 pounds by my thirteenth birthday. Yes, the nutritionist taught me what was good food and bad, what made a good protein combination, and how many calories were in certain fast food meals. I also learned to be constantly aware of what I was eating, the amount of calories in the food, and how much I weighed.

As children, the largest influences in our lives are our parents and family. If parents are constantly dieting and talking about unwanted weight or body aspects, the child will receive conscious and unconscious messages about their own body weight and image. If a parent conveys the importance of being thin, attractive, and at the perfect weight, then the message for the child is that the only way to be loved is to have those attributes. A single comment a parent makes can show the child that being thin is the only way to be loved.

It is important for parents to be aware of what they are saying to their kids about fat, dieting, and body image. Usually kids remember what you say when they might not even understand what "obese" or "chubby" really means. You need to be careful about what you say and how you talk to your kids about having a positive body image as well as eating healthy.

Friends

Teenagers are cruel to each other, especially when it comes to the way we look.

Here is an all too common scenario: Two girls have been best friends for a couple of years. They are both pretty girls with good grades and a lot of friends. One of the girls is a little bit thinner than the other. At a party guys hit on her more often than the best friend. The best friend feels left out, inadequate, and less in every way than her best friend. The only reason the "lesser" of the two friends can find for the reason she doesn't get as much attention from boys is because she is heavier. The five pound difference together with some little curves in a few different places turns her into, "I am fat."

Teenagers hate to be left out. They hate to feel inadequate and unworthy. When the opposite sex hits on a friend more often than you, you can feel left out. When a friend is able to wear clothes you cannot wear without showing bulges, you feel inadequate. When a friend makes it onto the basketball team and you don't, you feel unworthy. It happens all the time. If teenagers already have seeds of body image problems planted in them from childhood, eating and self-esteem problems grow when they are compared to friends. Even if they didn't have these seeds, the importance society places on the attractiveness of a person's body is absorbed by the minds of teenagers.

Teenagers compare their bodies to their friends even though we are told time after time, "Everyone's body is different." Honestly, the science of understanding why one girl's hips are bigger than her friend's has no significance to the "fat" girl—all she cares about is that her friend can wear the tightest dress, get the best guys, and still eat pizza for dinner.

The Media

According to most of the teenagers I interviewed, the media was not the biggest factor in their self-esteem problems. Almost all of them said that if they could, they would change more than one thing about their bodies. And every single one said that they had some sort of self-esteem problem ranging from an actual eating disorder to thinking compulsively about the way they look compared to others. They said the media was <u>not</u> the most important factor influencing their mindsets about their bodies. Rather, they said the media simply sets the precedent for how we judge each other and to what extent. Here are some of the responses I got when I asked them what they thought the influence of the media was on their self-esteem and body image:

A seventeen-year-old boy's response:

> "Oh, the media, you mean like the movies or magazines or what?"
> Question clarification: "All of those things."
> "Oh, well, I don't like watch a movie and go, 'I want to have that guy's body.' But when I am working out and am trying to motivate myself to go to the gym, I think about how the fat guys in movies are always the stupid, unattractive ones who end up watching while their friends get all of the girls. And I think, I don't want to be one of the fat ones." (Note: This guy was not fat … not even close.)

A seventeen-year-old girl's response:

> "Well, doesn't everyone look at like actresses and think, 'I want to look like them?' It's not even like I am watching a movie, and I think about having Jennifer Lopez's body. Well, I mean I do, but, it's mostly like in my magazines there will be this entire section on how to get Halle Berry's arms, Heather Locklier's abs, and Demi Moore's legs. I mean, it's one thing to see it on screen and leave it alone, but magazines, TV specials, and my friends push it on teens and say, 'Don't just watch it. Do it.' How am I supposed to let that not influence my self-esteem and body image!?"

A fifteen-year-old boy's response:

"Yeah, I mean I guess the movies influence my self-esteem, but mostly, you know, I hear my friends and other girls talking about how they love the guys in movies with nice arms and stomachs and stuff. Then I look at my arms and abs, and I think, you know, shit."

Magazines like <u>Seventeen</u> and <u>YM</u> are overflowing with articles on how to be thinner and more toned, how to have prettier hair and longer leg muscles. I think it is important to show teenagers how to take care of their bodies and become healthier. Just like my experience with the nutritionist, teenagers also need to be shown limits and reality.[2]

In this generation, eating disorders and obsessions with the body are not only found in girls. In fact, the level of eating disorders in boys is on the rise. Girls worry about being thin. They diet, throw up after meals, and count calories. Boys worry about the presence of flab. They worry about being thin *and* being muscular. Many boys now take steroids to perform better in sports and to become more muscular for the sake of body image and appearance. They take laxatives to lose weight. They even dabble in the thousands of over-the-counter products for bulking up, thinning down, and toning.

More and more teenagers are also considering plastic surgery. There are at least 26 teenagers I know personally who have had or who are about to have some sort of plastic surgery. I am not talking about just a nose job. Here are some of the more popular surgeries my female teenage interviewees have had: complete face reconstructive surgery, chin tucks, forehead lifts, breast implants and liposuction. Popular surgeries for boys include: breast reduction surgery, calf implants, ear pinning, and liposuction. All of the teenagers I talked to who have had plastic surgery or who were planning on surgery were below the age of 18.

Personally, I am not against cosmetic surgery. I believe that if a person wants to get something done that isn't too extreme, and it will help their self-esteem, they should be able to do it. The problem in most cases is it is not done out of necessity or even out of a true perception of reality or desire. Many of the girls and boys I talked to had plastic surgery done because their parents had money and encouraged them to do it.

One girl I know had her face completely redone. She was not an ugly girl before, and she looked completely different and a little bit odd after she had

2. Parent and teen tips on dealing with body image can be found in the next Section's Tips.

recovered from the surgery. When I asked her why she did it, she said, "Why not?"

Why not?

This, I thought to myself, is the result of a society obsessed with finding dissatisfaction in themselves.

The Opposite Sex

Homework, college pressures, and the intense desire to have friends and be liked are clearly teenage stressors, but the opposite sex is and always has been one of the greatest influences on teenage behavior and feelings of self worth.

In *school* the pressure to be funny in class, get good grades, be the smartest or even get the worst grades, depending on the atmosphere, can all depend on the opposite sex. Aside from the actual performance on tests and in class, the process of developing the persona you need to attract the opposite sex in school and after school is tremendously stressful. Many times teenagers, who will put up with the pressure from their parents to do well in school just to impress a member of the opposite sex, will make jokes in class and be scolded by the teacher. This pressure over impressing the opposite sex takes attention away from what school is all about. An atmosphere of learning becomes a battleground for attention, a show of wits and personality, and a scene for the dating game.

Not only do teens focus on attracting the opposite sex and who is dating whom, but there is also competition among your own sex for dates, including repercussions for dating certain people. Teenagers can be scorned for dating someone inside their group, (because a friend has dated that person previously), for dating outside their group, (because they have different friends and the group feels the disloyalty), or for not dating anyone at all. Talk about pressure no matter what you do!

Friends can also be incredibly hard to please when it comes to people you like, people you are dating, and people you want to date. Teenagers not only have to please their parents with their choice of partners, they must also please their friends. Yet with friends, it goes beyond the person you are dating. Jealousy issues cloud relations with the opposite sex and other teenagers. Teenage girls, especially, make issues around the opposite sex a particularly pressure-filled aspect of life. In the dating section you will read some personal stories concerning the jealousy, hatred, and revenge that wreak havoc on friendships.

A stare you get in the hallway, a name you were called when you were little, or a "What the Opposite Sex Really Likes" article in a magazine can trigger huge *self-esteem* issues. A couple of months ago, skinny girls and lanky boys were in.

Last week curvy girls and muscular men were in. This week, the perfect middle range of sizes is in. Never fat girls, flabby boys, or love handles.

I read a magazine article once that classified the different shapes of girls (pear, hour glass, banana or apple) and then described what type of guy (carrot, bell pepper, zucchini or squash) would like them the best. These were actually the names of the categories. Are you kidding me? If I actually followed that article, I would have a zucchini for a boyfriend. One friend told me, "In movies, the fat girl always plays the popular girl's best friend. The ugly 'curvaceous' girls never seem to get the guy, and it seems like all the girls in the movies who are above a size six are considered fat."

The *media* does exaggerate the body image and opposite sex stereotype, yet serious self-esteem issues are generated from the words and actions which come from the teens themselves. For example, if a group of guys goes around talking about how big butts are disgusting, you can bet the girls who hear them are going to do extra butt extensions that week. Especially if they are a younger teenager, they will think they have a big butt, and big butts will be forever unattractive. I know my best guy friend was fine with his body until he heard girls outside of a movie theater making fun of one of the guys in the movie and his squishy stomach. My friend overheard the girls talking about how grossed out they were, and he immediately started doing ab workouts everyday, even though his stomach was fine. Overall, most of the teens I interviewed said the need to impress the opposite sex probably had the biggest effect on self-esteem and positive body image.

The opposite sex has the biggest effect on a person's self-esteem, and the opposite sex can be the sole factor in deciding whether or not it is cool to study or speak out in class. Constant pressure to impress others is stressful and makes for a moody, anxious teen. A teenager's whole persona and self image may be crafted out of the pressure to impress others.

The Same Sex*

A huge source of pressure for teenagers of this generation is coming out and announcing their homosexuality. Because it is becoming more and more acceptable in the media and in society to be gay, many teens are coming out and/or dealing with their friends and families coming out. Yet, in many places in America and around the world, being gay is unaccepted and scorned. Some of my friends who are gay say the hardest part about coming out is not telling parents or friends, but the response they receive from people who find out second hand about their homosexuality. Looking at the news, we can see society's callousness in accepting this lifestyle and preference of homosexuality.

In October of 2002, the Gay/Straight Alliance at my high school in Los Angeles put on a brilliant performance to demonstrate the hardship gay and straight teens face. Before being able to perform the scenarios they put together in an all school assembly, the Gay/Straight Alliance had to fight a battle with the school.

The high school I attended was and is a wonderful all-girl school. It is very liberal in its beliefs and student programs, but it also has strict rules and traditions. It enrolls grades seven through twelve and has an amazing faculty and campus. Not many high school students can say that they love their school, but I honestly can say that I loved mine. Yet, even as much as I loved my high school, I felt that the decision it made with the encouragement of certain seventh and eighth grade parents concerning the Gay/Straight Alliances assembly was horrific.

The Alliance planned and submitted a script for the all-school assembly. The administration, at the requests of many parents, decided the material was too adult for the seventh and eighth grade students and barred them from the assembly. Yes, that is correct. The school did not allow them to attend unless they had a signed permission slip from their parents. I and other students in the school thought that was absolutely ludicrous. How could it be that the younger students were forbidden to go to the assembly when they themselves were **in** the club? How is it the administration forbade the younger students from going to the assembly when these same students saw members of the Gay/Straight Alliance everyday in the hallways holding hands? Should they not understand some of their feelings and the prejudices to which they were subjected as a result of their homosexuality?

How were the younger students who had feelings of homosexuality to respond when they were told the assembly on the subject was inappropriate for them? By not allowing the younger students into the assembly, the school sent the message that something was wrong or "inappropriate" with being a homosexual. The decision not to allow the younger students into the assembly simply promoted intolerance and ignorance among the students.

A couple of weeks after the assembly my school celebrated Halloween. The seniors, as a class theme, decided to come as gay seventh and eighth graders to make a statement to the school. The administration found out, and we were forbidden to dress as gay seventh and eighth graders. The administration felt that we would be mocking the school's authority.

How could they think that?

This is just one example of how homosexuality can be treated with fear and intolerance. For a homosexual teen, the pressure is great, and intolerance by friends only increases the stress.

With the permission of the Marlborough School Gay/Straight Alliance, I am printing here the scenes acted out at the school assembly from which the seventh and eighth graders were excluded. You will see the daily hardships and lifestyle issues that gays and their families endure. You will also see that the assembly was completely appropriate and overall a very influential lesson in tolerance.

Today we, with the help of the members of our club, have put together an assembly that will hopefully open your eyes to something new. The Gay/Straight Alliance is part of Marlborough. It's a part of you, and it's a part of me. I could only **begin** *to describe us by using the words gay, straight, lesbian, bisexual, transgender, open, questioning, oppressed, and hiding. The Alliance is not composed of only one sexual orientation. Our purpose is to try to promote tolerance of all sexual orientations. We represent all of you. And today, we offer you this. We offer you understanding. We are not afraid of you. We are always open, and we will always be here for you. And in return for all of this, we ask simply that you listen to us, even if you cannot accept us. We ask you to try to understand the things that the Alliance stands for. Our door is always open, and if you have the chance, we welcome you to any of our meetings. Thank you.*

Every day, kids and adults around the world have to deal with embarrassment, hate, fear, confusion and a million other things because they are not straight. Now, though, we're going to change things up a bit, and see what it would be like if the world were switched around; if the straight people feared others knowing who they were, if you girls were expected to find a nice girl or else you weren't considered normal. And while it may seem completely absurd, think about the fact that this is really what kids our age go through all the time. We appreciate your respect, and hope you enjoy. Thank you.

Scene 1

Family is seated at table, eating breakfast. Two MOMs and SISTER are happily eating, talking, etc. GIRL sits poking her food, silent.

Mom: *Honey, I hear there's a dance this weekend. Are you taking Jessica?*

Sister: *(smiling) Yeah, she asked me last night.*

Mom 2: *That's lovely, dear. (To GIRL) How about you, honey? Have you asked anyone?*
(GIRL shakes head, silent)

Sister: *You know, if you want, I can set you up with someone. I know a lot more girls than you, and there's one girl in my bio class who's been asking about you …*

Mom: *Ooooh. You should ask her. There's no reason a pretty girl like you shouldn't have lots of girls after you …*
(GIRL drops her spoon, looks up. Everyone is silent.)

GIRL: *Look, stop. Mom, Mommy, I've got to talk to you. (To Sister) You may as well hear it, too. (Deep breath) I'm straight … I've been dating this boy named Brian for … a little over a month. I've known for a while now. And … yeah. I'm straight.*
(Mom pushes chair away and exits, angry and upset)

Mom 2: *Oh, honey. I … Are you sure? I mean, you're only 16, maybe you're just confused, experimenting. You're so young, I'm sure you'll grow out of it once you grow up a bit. Maybe it's because we put you in a co-ed school, having all those boys around, the way some of the teachers flaunt it as if, well, as if it were normal. I still love you, honey, of course, but you know it's not normal to like boys.*

Sister: *No way. I always thought you were weird, I didn't think you were straight. That's so gross. You mean you've actually kissed a boy?*
(Mom comes back in, angry)

Mom: *I'm not having a straight person in my house. I have a number for a, a doctor. A therapist. She can help you get … better, get over this stupid idea you have. If you don't, though, if you want to go ahead with that … disgusting lifestyle, go ahead, but you cannot stay in this house. I will not have that in my family.*

GIRL: *I love him, though, that's all. It's not like I chose to like guys …*

Mom: *(interrupting) I don't want to hear it. I'm going to work now. I can't deal with this. Goodbye.*

BLACKOUT

<u>SCENE 1</u>

A group of girls sit on couch, watching TV, eating popcorn, etc.

Brianna: *Can someone remind me why we're watching this? This show is idiotic. Give me the remote. (Reaches for remote from B)*

Liza: *(keeping it from her) No way. Tom Welling is soo hot!*

Melissa: *Which one is he?*

Liza: *Superman!*

Melissa: *Oh yeah. He's cute, but I like the guy who plays Lex Luther better.*

Brianna: *Ok, one, that's gross. He's bald. Two, I'm not watching this dumb show. It sucks. The whole WB is gay. Gimme the remote! (reaches for remote again)*
(Jules, who had been formerly silent, looks up at this)

Jules: *FREEZE!*

(All freeze where they were. D stands up and continues)

The show is idiotic, dumb. It sucks. So the word you use is gay. Well I'm gay. So what does that mean about me? I'd call you on it, but you'd say …

Brianna: *(Unfreezing momentarily) I don't actually mean <u>gay</u>. It's just a word. It's like, the meaning has changed … (Freezes again)*

Jules: *But it doesn't stop the fact that you use that word. I'm not stupid, or idiotic, or bad. I'm just gay.*

Jules sits back down BLACKOUT

I want to thank Annalee Fannan, Rachel Dearborn, and Roach Janken for allowing me to publish this performance. The students and faculty at Marlborough loved the assembly. It had a huge impact on the way people thought about homosexuals, and it changed behavior in the student body, such as the indiscriminate use of the word gay. The seventh and eighth graders will probably not be able to come to any future Alliance assemblies unless someone or something changes significantly, and that, in my opinion, is a true loss for them.

A Twist

Is it hip to come out? With schools, many institutions, and parents trying to block the liberty of homosexuality, many teenagers are coming out … stylishly.

I went on a website recently which allowed Internet surfers to rate other people who put their pictures and stats on the Internet. My brother's friend added his name and information to the hundreds of other people logged in on the website. If you are interested in someone's picture and information, you can send them your stats to see if they want to meet you. I am not a big fan of Internet dating, but I humored my brother and looked at the girls who were interested in his friend. Here are two of them:

Name:	Alexis Brown*
Age:	22
Description:	I have blonde hair and green eyes. I am a bisexual and love brunettes. I love playing basketball and reading.
Name:	Talia Gent*
Age:	19
Description:	I am a bisexual, and I love to surf and hang out with my friends. I love French fries.

*names changed

There were six girls listed on his page, and every single one of them said that they were bisexuals except one. Hmmmmm.... I thought it was interesting that they were all bisexual. I started looking at the descriptions of other girls on the website, and almost ALL of them were bisexual! A couple of girls I actually know were logged into the network, and when I looked them up, they also said they were bisexual. I decided to call and ask them about it, saying that I had no idea they were bisexual and wondering why they hadn't told me. They mostly said, "Oh, no, I am not bisexual, but guys are more intrigued by bisexuals. Besides it's the 'in' thing to be bisexual." The only thing I could think to respond was, "Oh, right." Whether it is the "in" thing or not, many teenagers, especially teenage girls, are coming out, and slowly the movement is gaining more acceptance.

External Pressure

"I hate going to dinners with friends of my parents, they always ask me about school and my goals, and all I want to do is run to the bathroom because I don't even know yet, what am I supposed to tell them?"
  -Teenager, 16

Whether the pressure is coming from our parents, our friends or ourselves, we constantly find ourselves living up to other people's expectations and judgments.

I remember once I was in a coffee shop comforting one of my upset girlfriends who was crying and distressed. A nosy woman at the next table turned in her seat and barged in on our private conversation. "Now what pressure could you teenagers possibly be under? Stop that crying, you don't even know what stress is yet," she chirped at us, admonishing and criticizing at the same time. I turned to the rather rude women and responded, "Well, tell us, what are _you_ stressed about?" She looked at me rather quizzically and proceeded to tell me and my crying friend about her job issues and her family problems and her constant worrying about money. After she was done and we had listened patiently to her story, I said to her, "I understand that you are under a lot of stress. Now, you try to imagine living a life where you are constantly worried if you are good enough. You are constantly worried if you will make it successfully through six more years of school, whether you will get a good job, whether you will be able to raise a family of your own and be able to support it. And then think for a minute about how you will get there. How much more school? How good will your performance be? Good enough? Imagine trying to deal with new situations and interact with people, trying to be cool while your voice is changing or you are getting boobs." I paused, more for dramatic effect then for a breath, and I finished, "With all of that, imagine having your parents looming over you, reminding you about college, having your friends compete with you for the best grade, outfit, or crush. And most of all, imagine having people tell you that you are not really stressed and that teenage issues do not really matter."

She looked at me and was quiet for a moment, trying to take in what I had just said. Then she said simply, "Hmm, I never thought about it that way," and proceeded to finish her cup of coffee.

Teenage issues should matter, to our parents and to all other adults, because they matter to teenagers. It is important to realize the effect adults and strangers can have on the packed teenage mind.

Excuse me, do I know you?

Tips on Conversations with Teenagers and Trap Topics

I cannot tell you the number of times I have been asked my GPA, my SAT scores, or where I am going to apply to college by acquaintances and/or total strangers. It seems the only requirement needed for someone to ask you about college or grades or scores is the fact that you go to high school. Sometimes as teenagers, when we attempt to go out on a run, get mail from the mailbox, or go to the supermarket for parents, we are rudely reminded of things that already stress us out. A great deal of the pressure put on us does not only come from people close to us, but also from strangers and acquaintances who believe it is perfectly okay for them to comment on our lives.

I believe adults suppose the college process is the only common ground they have with teenagers for conversation purposes. After all, many adults went to high school, graduated, and had their own slew of test scores and college applications. Because of this, the only topic of conversation these adults seem to think they have with teenagers revolves around school and our futures. However, that is one of the reasons there are so many problems between adults and teenagers. A teenage stereotype of grown adults is that they only want to nag and push young adults around. Even if the adult doesn't mean to be pushy and is just curious about a teen's ambitions, or more commonly, the adult has nothing else to talk about, the mention of the school based topic becomes fatal.

The school based interaction becomes problematic in two ways. First, it puts teenagers on the defensive. When a random adult talks to us about something on which our parents harp at home or with which our college counselors bombard us at school, we immediately, out of habit, go into a defensive mode. Our instinct is to be independent, and when any adult or stranger brings up a possible curb on our independence or a subject about which we already feel pressure, we will not be able to relate to that person, and we only resent them for bringing up the dreaded topic. Second, school is not really a subject of interest for the teenager or the adult. Just because school makes up a major part of your life as a young adult does not mean that any young adult wants to talk about it. One can assume the teen and the adult are not very close. One can assume this, because, if they were, the adult would already know the answers to the questions. Because of this lack of connection, the adult does not care about a teenager's SAT score, unless the adult is planning on judging the teen. This is another reason the conversation can make the teen uncomfortable, because the teen knows some judgment or other thought is forthcoming from this stranger who perceives it as just making conversation.

For Adults and Teens*

> To prevent uncomfortable and resentment provoking conversations with teenagers, try to avoid anything you think causes them stress. This also goes for teenagers when meeting new people or trying to make conversations with old friends. By avoiding stressful topics, you lessen the chance of being uncomfortable and/or making the other person feel inadequate or judged.

Here are some ideas and topics to bring up while in conversation with teenagers. These also work great as conversation starters:

1.   Have they seen any of the new movies or TV shows?

2.   What kinds of activities do they enjoy?

3.   Which clubs and/or groups do they enjoy at school?

4.   Do they play sports in school?

5.   Which sports do they watch on TV? Favorite teams?

These topics tend to be pretty neutral and interesting to talk about for teenagers and adults.

Tricks to Help Relieve Pressure

"What am I supposed to talk about? Oh, I don't know, anything that they like. I usually stick to whatever sports game was on last night."
-Uncle, 28, when asked about how he talks to his nephews

There are tons of books, internet websites, and advice columns that list ways to get closer to your teenager as well as ways for a teenager to develop a better relationship with his or her parents. Doctors, adults, and parents write tips of advice for adults to give to other adults that never actually benefit or make a difference to most teenagers. I gave some teens I interviewed adult books with tips to give to parents about getting along better with their teens. Here are some of the tips and what teens had to say about them:

1. **For parents: "Talk about yourself sometimes instead of the teen.** They hate to be the only topic under discussion. Tell them about your own teen memories and mistakes."

   RESPONSES:

   — "Are you kidding me? Sure, I don't always like to be the topic of discussion, but to hear my parents' old stories that I have heard about a thousand times, that is a great way to teach your teen how to tune out."
   Female, 16

   —This guy just laughed ... for about two minutes ... while he shook his head.
   Male, 17

2. **"Set-up and use family meetings to full advantage.** Get input from each person about rules, curfews, etc., as well as the consequences of breaking rules. Sign agreements, try them out; modify as needed."

RESPONSES:

—"The last thing I need to be doing is signing a piece of paper that says when my curfew is. And my parents don't listen to me anyway. I would be signing a piece of paper that solidifies THEIR curfew time not my desired curfew time."
Male, 16

—"I hate those family meetings. Ummmm … waste of my time. We sit around and argue about rules or the decisions that my parents have *already made*. Yeah, that's helpful to me."
Female, 14

These were just two of the many pieces of horrible advice given to parents about how to forge better relationships with their teenagers. In the next couple of pages, I will give advice to both teens and parents about how to improve their relationship with far better results.

The reason most of the parent/teen tips are in the "Pressure Section" is because the parent/teen relationship IS a huge source of pressure. A teen's relationship with his or her parents affects everything in the teen's life. If a teen does not get along with parents, it affects when and where the teen can go out with friends, who and when they can date, how much support they get in school … everything. All of these tips are separated into categories and can be used by both parents and teens.

To put these tips into action, there does not need to be a family meeting or anything of the sort, but only an acknowledgement of a problem or future problems so that both parties can try to work to fix it in their own ways.

Two important points I mentioned here make up the first two important rules or tips for constructing a relationship. The first thing to know for both the parents and the teenagers is this:

BOTH the parent and teen have to acknowledge that there is a problem with the relationship … if there is one. Parents and teens should read this book to prevent problems in the future.

If there is a barrier, resentment, or punishment involved in your relationship, then both the teen and the parent need to be ready to make a change. I am a teenager, and I know that even when the parent wants to make the change, teens often do not. This is ok. The parent or adult can begin to take these steps until the teen is ready. Maybe with the effort

the parent puts in, the relationship will get better, and the teen <u>will</u> be motivated to make the change.

For parents to get the ball rolling toward a better relationship with their teen, these are the Golden Rules:

1) Don't push and don't nag.

These rules should be applied to every single one of the rules in this book. It is the most important by far. No matter what you ask of your teen, you are guaranteed to get a better result if you do not add pushing or nagging. That's right. If you only apply one rule from this entire book, let it be this one. I promise you the thing teens hate the most are parents that nag and push them to do things they do not *want* to do. I know many teenagers, including me, who have changed their minds about something they actually wanted to do simply because their parents nagged them to do it. Parents are much better off suggesting, encouraging, and hinting rather than pushing, nagging, and forcing.

Teenagers hate when you push them to clean their rooms, nag them to go to their grandma's house, or mind their table manners. You cannot push the idea of communication and openness. <u>Communication and openness require a process which happens over time with nurturing, respect, and patience. Communication and openness are the ultimate goals for a parent/teen relationship.</u>

2) Positive Reinforcement.

I will start this rule off with an example. When I was young, before school I would make eggs in the microwave in a cup. It was quick, easy, and tasty. One problem, sometimes the egg would pop or explode if I overcooked it. Often times little bits or spills would cling to the walls, ceilings, or bottom of our microwave. I would usually mop most of it up with a paper towel, but since I was getting ready for school and very hungry, sometimes I would miss little bits. My stepmom got very mad at me and **pushed** and **nagged** me (the number one "no-no") to clean it up again. She nagged me so much that I would sometimes purposely not clean it well because it made me mad that it made her so mad. Finally, every time I did clean the microwave, she would say thank you so much for cleaning the microwave, "I really appreciate it." That made me happy and feel good, so I started to wipe it out always.

So replace your pushing and nagging. Every time your teen does something positive, like pick up a piece of laundry or clean his room without asking, tell them how much you appreciate it and give them a hug or allow them another half hour of TV. I guarantee that the lack of nagging and negative consequences, replaced by positive reinforcements and rewards, will be the motivation to do whatever it is that's desired. Also, it is much easier to reward than it is to punish and nag. Doesn't all that punishing and nagging get tiring?

Communication

3) Be accessible, flexible, and willing,

This is a tough one, and to be completely honest, most teenagers cannot do it. That is why it is crucial for parents who are dealing with disgruntled and closed-up teens to be the ones who start it and model it.

- Accessibility—If you have a teenager who doesn't talk to you or others very often, or even a teenager about whom you think you know everything, always be available to listen to them. As long as you don't push your accessibility, this can be a gift to some teenagers. When a parent is always available to listen and help out unexpectedly, a teen feels heard and valued. This does not necessarily mean a parent should give advice. Just listen. That allows the teen to feel less intimidated.

- Flexibility—Teenagers often want to discuss and talk about issues at odd and sometimes inconvenient times. Sometimes it is necessary to be there even if the time isn't so convenient.

- Willingness—Your teenager will not talk to you no matter how accessible and flexible you are if you are not willing to listen without JUDGMENT. If you are willing to give your teenager advice without making judgments about what they are saying, then the teenager will be able to express worries more freely, feel less self-conscious, and trust you more.

There are many benefits to being accessible, flexible and willing. The first is your teen will know they have an outlet to express concerns, excitement, or daily events. The second is the teenager becomes more open, and with the openness, the teenager himself feels better and freer. The third, and one of the most important benefits of being accessible, flexible and open to your teenager, is that you will get to understand what is really happening in your teen's mind and forge a deeper and more powerful long term relationship that gets closer over time, even into adulthood.

4) Be a wall.

Ok, I know this sounds horrible, but it is very important in communicating with a teenager. There are a few components:

- Don't always give advice. Talking about our problems is a way of expressing ourselves. It is also a way in which we work out our problems. Just by putting it out into the air, we can get it off our chests, and that alone can help solve the problem. Even though I am sure you have plenty of wonderful advice for your teenager on love, dealing with teachers and friends, and other issues, sometimes it can be more destructive to offer up advice. I would say a parent should not give advice, especially lengthy lectures, unless and until it is asked for by the teen. Just give emotional support. Listen with your heart, not your head. Sometimes it may seem what your teen is saying is not relevant, important, or necessarily good, but you need to feel the suffering, upset, or excitement as if the events happened to you. Murmur things like, "That's rough," or "I am so sorry," or "Wow, how upsetting," or "That must be shocking," or whatever is appropriate. Active listening without advice is key. There is a big difference between advice and emotional support for a teen.

- Don't pry. Resist the urge to need to know everything that is going on in your teenager's life. It is great to be interested, but it is bad to be pushy. Asking too many questions about what a teenager is doing can be dangerous. The teenager can take it as invasive and distrusting behavior and will, therefore, shut down to further communication.

- Be supportive. You will see in the next section ways that a parent can be supportive of their teenager.

5) Things to say and not to say.

The following do's and don't's apply to regular conversations with teens and outline good lifestyle patterns that teenagers would do well to learn for their own futures.

<u>DO'S</u>

1. Give lots of positive feedback. Teenagers love to hear praise and encouragement just as we all do. Sometimes, a few positive words can really up our self-esteem and let us know that you are paying attention to us.

2.   Do give us some credit. We are not little kids, and even though we do not always carry through on our responsibilities, it is important to give us responsibilities that allow us to make our own decisions.

DON'T'S

1.   Don't confuse the friend/parent role. It is great to be a shoulder to lean on and a confidant, but it is not good to lose the authority you should and need to have over your teenager. The parents' job is to protect their children. Parents must remember they do not always have to agree with what their teens are doing and must say no.

2.   It is important to tell your kids about your issues and problems, but do not place your problems on them. Honestly, it sucks that parents are obliged to listen to our problems with cliques and friends, but most teenagers don't care about the details of your meetings at work or your problems with your own friends.

3.   Don't belittle a teenager's problems. There have been many times when I have told an adult a problem I am having, and that adult says things like this in response:

"You're just a kid—what do you have to worry about?"

"Don't worry, you'll get through it. Besides…."

"You don't have it hard. When I was a kid…. And right now I am going through…."

This is the WORST thing an adult can do when a teenager is telling the adult about a problem. It demonstrates you not only don't care about what is going on with us, but you also think you are more important than we are, and that what matters to us does not really matter to you at all.

6) Don't break a promise or confidence.

It is really important to respect your teenager's privacy and space. This includes knocking on doors <u>before</u> you enter a room, not picking up the extension phone when your teen is on the phone, and not going into your teen's room when you have not been given consent. A breach of privacy can be disastrous for a teenage/parent relationship. If a teenager feels that his or her space or confidence has been crossed or violated, they will lose respect and trust in the parent.

REMEMBER: If you breach a teens' trust and privacy by snooping and/or trying to find things out, you will end up finding out less in the long run because they will not have the trust to tell you. You will find much more through trust and communication than you ever will under the bed or in a desk drawer.

Action

7) Find common interests and do them.

Common hobbies and interests are great ways to spend time and get to know your teenager. Just make sure it is really a common interest and that you are not *pushing* your teenager into hanging out with you.

8) Invite your teenager's friends over to your house.

It might seem a little daunting to have five or six teenagers come over after school, watch TV in your living room, eat through the cabinets in your kitchen, and blare music upstairs, but at least you know what they are doing. It is better to have the teenagers eating and being loud at your house than smoking in the alley or hanging out at the home of someone you do not know.

My mom and dad are always hugely welcoming to my friends. I am always able to bring all of my friends over, as long as I follow some of the house rules. Those rules include: cleaning up after ourselves; not being overly loud; common respect for the house and the other inhabitants in the house; and, if you use up food or other items, leave a list of what needs replacing so it's there for everyone else when they want it.

It is great to have Halloween parties at my house and invite my friends over after school. Here are some reasons to allow your teenager to invite friends over:

- You know what your teenager is doing and where he or she is.

- You get a chance to meet your teenager's friends. (Can be crucial when it comes to partying and going out rules.)

- Your teenager will appreciate your generosity and open house policy.

REMEMBER: It is your house, and you have to make sure you set ground rules for your teenager and his or her friends.

9) Some physical closeness isn't bad.

Despite disagreements on this issue with some of my friends, I think physical closeness is important. Hugs, pats on the shoulder, and neck rubs show us teenagers that you love us and that you care. BUT make sure you aren't pushy with your physical affection. This can cause teenagers to pull away.

When Asserting Authority

10) If you are going to lecture.

I am a teenager, and I hate to be lectured to, but as an authority figure, parents need to assert their authority.

- Tell Them Why.

When making decisions about curfew or what your teenager can and can't do, make sure you give them a good reason. The "do it because I said you need to" and "just because" reasons for your decisions make teens resentful and angry. Always give reasons behind the no answer. If there is really no reason to say no, then should you really be saying no?

- Compromise.

When dealing with a rule or issue, try to make some sort of compromise with your teenager, because there will be plenty of times when your teenager does not have any input. If there is an appropriate situation for teen input, ask for it. Your teen will appreciate it and will feel valued and respected. Taking your teens' opinions and needs into consideration when making decisions that concern them shows them that you care about their thoughts.

- Speak your mind.

Believe it or not, we do listen to parents. If the lecture is not a punishment speech, but rather a talk with meaningful dialogue, (both sides must speak), we will listen, especially on the sensitive and difficult issues, e.g., sex, drugs, success. Have a talk, not a punishment speech. During the talk, speak your mind and say what you think about the subject. Try not to make it too long or too sappy. Teenagers do listen to their parents, even if they don't admit it. Just make sure not to push whatever your ideas are onto your teenagers. Simply telling them with good reasons is enough for us to hear your point, and maybe, just maybe, believe it ourselves.

• Don't be duped.

Teenagers lie to their parents, whether the lies are big or small. Make sure you search for the truth before accepting everything your teenager says. If they feel like they can trick you, they will lose all respect for you and your rules and constantly hide the truth.

Body Image and Your Teen's Self-Esteem

11) Don't ever call your teenager (or anyone for that matter) stupid.

It happens all the time, especially with little kids. The child drops a plate or gets a problem wrong on that night's homework, and the parent barks, "You're so stupid. You little shit. Look what you did, you idiot." Really encouraging. Parents, as I have said before, have huge influences in a developing a teen's feelings of self-worth.

12) Compliment your teenager.

Compliments let your teen know you care and make your teenager feel good, even if they act as if they don't hear them.

13) Never tease your teenager about their body or intelligence.

This goes right along with never telling your child that his or her problems are insignificant. Commenting on weight, what your teen is eating, or clothing size can be devastating for self-esteem.

14) Notice what messages you are sending out about your own body.

I know from personal experience as well as from what other teens tell me that having someone around you who is constantly dieting and hating their body can make you look at your own weight and body in a skewed fashion. Comments about your teenagers' friend's bodies and/or actresses and actors can also have a negative effect on how teenagers feel about themselves.

15) Talk about health just as seriously as you talk about sex.

Yes, I think there should be a health talk. Many young adults and teenagers do not know what healthy eating is. It is extremely important to talk to your teenager or child about what is healthy and what is not. Take them to the supermarket and explain what a balanced diet is and how often a person should exercise. If you yourself do not know all of the aspects of a healthy diet, please refer to the contacts in the back of this book for a nutritionist and for resources for information.

Unfortunately teens are extremely high maintenance. I hope these tips help. Below I have provided an overview list of all the tips mentioned above. The condensed form can be easier to follow, carry around, review, and consult for reminders if and when the need arises.

<u>Overview List for Parents</u>

How to Improve Your Relationship with Your Teenager

- Don't push or nag.

- Be easily available and flexible to listen.

- Don't make judgments about your teenager's lifestyle or problems.

- Don't give advice unless it is requested.

- Don't pry.

- Be supportive by giving advice when requested; always give unsolicited positive feedback even on the little things.

- Give teens a level of responsibility which allows them to make their own decisions.

- Don't blend the parent/friend line; keep your authority.

- Don't bog down your teen with too many of your problems.

- Don't breach your teenager's privacy.

- Find some common interests.

- Encourage your teenager to invite friends over to your home.

- A hug is good.

- Don't belittle your teenager's needs and problems.

- Give the reasons behind your decisions.

- Tell your teen in a direct and forthright manner (without preaching) what you think about drugs, sex, and other important issues in their lives.

- Don't always believe what your teenager says.

- Never comment on the weight or body of your teenager in a negative way.

- Teach your children about good health.

For Teenagers
Relieving Pressure

College and Our Futures

1) Make a plan

Even if you have no idea what you want to be or where you want to go in life, it is really important to know your goals and aspirations. Think of short term and long term goals and start writing them down. For everything from getting an "A" in math class to becoming a lawyer, realistic or not, start thinking about what you want out of life so you can make it a reality. Having goals and aspirations gives you motivation to work towards what you want. Also, don't worry about being realistic or not. You are young; be idealistic and write down everything you want out of your life or your ideal job. What you focus on expands. Great athletes improve their performance by visualizing the outcome before the competition begins. Teenagers can and should do the same thing.

Once you have your long and short-term goals set, start thinking about the how. How are you going to get there? You don't have to make an actual detailed lay-out of your future. As long as you start thinking about your future, you will feel less lost and more motivated.

REMEMBER: Don't pick goals that are overwhelming or <u>completely</u> unattainable since these can be debilitating rather than motivating.

2) College

College is one of those things on which I could write another book, but here are some basic tips to make this horrifying project seem a little less daunting.

- <u>Become knowledgeable about the process.</u>

   The college process is COMPLETELY ARBITRARY. Every year since seventh grade I watched as the seniors at my school cried, rejoiced, and debated the decisions that rolled in all at the same time. You could never guess who would get in where because the process is COMPLETELY ARBITRARY. I say arbitrary because a student can have perfect grades, do community service, and play a varsity sport and still not get into the school of choice. Because many top schools are becoming more and more selective, more and more deserving students are not getting accepted. *It is extremely important to go into the college process knowing that if you do not get into a particular school, it has nothing to do with your self-worth and everything to do with the college itself.*

* <u>Check out all of your options.</u>

In my sophomore year of high school, I started checking out colleges and universities, which I call college in this book as a shorthand. I visited all kinds of colleges, even ones to which I didn't think I would apply for admission. This was really important for me because it allowed me to see all my options and what was out there. By seeing all of the different types of schools with the different types of campuses, different types of students studying in different kinds of majors, I was able to see what was out there and learn what I really wanted in a school. Students should not only visit all types of colleges but also apply to a variety of different schools.

A friend of mine who is a year older decided to apply to one of each type of school, even though she thought she knew which kind of school she wanted to attend. She applied to one big school, one small school, one school on the East Coast, one school on the West Coast, one school in the Midwest, one liberal arts college, and several University of California campuses. Yes, she had to do a lot of applications, but when she finally had to make her decision in the spring, she had completely changed her mind about the type of school she wanted to attend. Luckily, she had applied to every type of school and had the options she needed since she was accepted by several of them. Even if you think you know what you want in a school, make sure to check out your options and apply to a variety of institutions.

* <u>Keep records.</u>

As you visit all of the different schools, make sure to keep notes on the good and bad qualities of each school. I had visited 45 campuses in the last two years of high school. Yes, that's right, 45 campuses. Talk about exploring different options! If I hadn't kept a notebook with each school's characteristics, I would never have been able to distinguish among them later when deciding where to apply. Additionally, make sure to keep track of all of your contacts with the schools to which you plan to apply. It will keep you organized in the flood of paperwork that comes along in junior and senior year.

- Apply.

There is no one piece of advice that can be given to students applying to college except to try to stay out of overwhelm and to be yourself. If a school cannot accept you for who you are, then you do not want to go there anyway.

School

3) Teachers

No one likes a teacher's pet, yet it does not pay to be the class clown. After talking to more than 45 teachers about their opinions about teenagers, many of them said knowing a student who works hard for their class makes them like and appreciate that student. In fact, most of the teachers with whom I spoke were less irritated with students (the common stereotype teenagers I interviewed had about what their teachers thought of them) and more interested. Mrs. Reid Cottingham answered my question about what she wanted to know most about teenagers with, "I would like to know who they are aside from who they think they should be."

4) Get Organized

Staying organized is the key to success in everything. Getting notebooks for each class with dividers and folders will help keep all papers organized so that they are easily accessible for later dates. Organize not only your class papers but also your time. Get an organizer planner and make sure you plan out all of the things you have to do in a day, including sports practices, homework, and doctors' appointments. This way you do not miss important appointments, and you will make it more likely that you will get all of your work done and still have some time for yourself.

REMEMBER: Always make sure you have free time for yourself and time to be with your friends. This time is just as crucial to your success and well being as homework or sports time is. Don't trade it away for extra studying or odd jobs.

5) Homework Binder

It might seem small, but my homework binder saved my life. In high school we have tons of classes, homework, and papers to organize and to have handy.

Our backpacks end up weighing more than we do by the time we get in all the books and notebooks that we need for each class. The homework binder became a great solution for me. Get a one inch or half inch binder and put two dividers in it with a notebook hole puncher. Put all your assignment sheets from each class into the front of the binder before the dividers. This way, you don't have to check all your notebooks to figure out your homework for the night.

You can also put all completed homework behind the first divider and the unfinished homework behind the second divider so you can keep all of your homework and papers organized in one place! The homework binder is also a great place to put notes which need to be signed by parents or reminders about events, because all of your papers are in one notebook you will carry around always. By keeping lined notebook paper in the back of the binder, you can also use it for emergency scratch paper if you need it.

The Relationship with Our Parents

I have given a whole bunch of advice to parents and adults for dealing with teenagers. Now it is our turn. There is some stuff, surprisingly, that we can do to get our parents to trust us more, to get along with our parents better, and to make our overall teenage experience a better one.

After talking to many parents about their relationships with their teenagers and about what they thought would make them better, and after talking to other teenagers about what they would and would not do to make their relationship with their parents better, I came up with a list of helpful hints for dealing with parents.

6) Let them know what is going on. Talk to your parents.

Parents love to know what is going on in our lives. Simply telling them about your day at school or the fight you got into with your math teacher can have a huge effect.

Here are some major incentives for talking to your parents:

1. They will feel as if they are getting to know you better, and they probably are.

2. As they feel they understand more about what goes on in your life, they will begin to trust you more. With this newly gained trust, they will allow you to go out and do more things.

3.   If you talk to your parents, you will probably be venting some stuff that is on your mind so you will end up feeling better.

4.   Believe it or not, parents can actually have some good advice. If you are having a problem, talking to them about it will not only achieve some of the things I have just mentioned, it also might even help you solve your problems.

7) Ask them what is going on.

Your parents have lives, too, and I am sure it goes beyond their own hobbies, errands, and meetings at the office. If they ask you how your day was, and you answer because of the benefits listed above, you can then ask them how <u>their</u> day was. Remember, if your Mom or Dad have big events going on, ask them how they are doing or how it went. This interest will show them that you have respect for them, and in return, they will have more respect for you.

Keep in mind parents love to tell stories. Ask them about what it was like when they were a teenager. Even if you have already heard the stories, some of the stuff can be pretty interesting, or at least the information can be used to make fun of them and tease them later.

8) Just tell them.

It might seem simple, but the reason many teenagers argued with me against talking to their parents was they were afraid their parents would "nosy in" on everything else in their lives. If you just feel like venting to your parents about your bad day, tell them, "I am just venting. All you have to do is listen." That will let them know that you don't want them to give you advice. Tell them you just want an active listener to hear you and witness your upset. That's all.

9) If you act like you are 10 years old, they will treat you like you are 10 years old.

This is pretty simple to understand, but hard enough to do. If you leave a mess all over the house, don't pick up after yourself, and/or fail to follow any of your parents' rules and chore responsibilities, then you cannot expect your parents to allow you to go out with friends and do whatever you want. <u>If you disrespect their rules, they will give you more rules. If you break the rules, they will not let you go out at all.</u>

An important piece of advice here is this. If you want to go out on a Saturday night, do all of your chores Saturday during the day, wash the dishes (even though you are not asked), and then ask your parents in a responsible manner. You might be wondering what that means. Here's an explanation.

Asking for Things

To ask responsibly is to tell your parents exactly what you will be doing, with whom, and when. Then you can start to discuss what time you think you should be able to come home. If your parents know where you are, and you give them good reasons for setting a reasonable curfew time, then you will most likely come to an agreement close to what you want.

What you don't want to do is blow up if your parents say no. After all, they are your parents. However, if this is not enough, remember the reason you don't want to blow up is because you definitely will not get your way this time and you probably will not get your way next time if you lose your temper.

10) Be honest.

As obvious as it sounds, the more honest you are, the less you will get into trouble. Keeping the trust with your parents is so important because they will feel more at ease when they really do know what is going on with you. Once you gain their trust, they are more likely to give you leeway in the future with your plans. It is bad to lie. You will most likely get caught. The road back to trust is tough, bumpy, and very unpleasant.

11) Don't just take out the garbage, wash the dishes, too.

Ok, so this is a good one. When I learned to do this, it made everything in the house easier. Besides actually doing the chores your parents assign to you, do a little extra. If you see some dirty dishes in the sink, wash them. If the laundry needs to be taken out and folded, do it while you watch TV, <u>without</u> your parents having to ask you. This tactic can be <u>very</u> effective, and it will probably end up saving you time in the long run. When you do extra chores, it:

#1—makes your parents happy because they have less work to do on top of their extremely busy lives;

#2—makes them appreciate you more so they nag you less later and might even let you have more privileges;

#3—is polite and respectful to your parents. Our parents do so much for us that we do not even realize or consider. These little considerate acts can help pay them back for, oh, let's say, some of the clothes, food, and shelter they have provided for you over the years.

Dealing with Parents in Arguments
Asking Permission and Getting into Trouble

12) Don't blow up … especially if *you* are the one who is wrong.

I see it all the time. My friend and his parents get in a small or medium fight about something, and my friend blows up and starts yelling about completely relevant and sometimes irrelevant issues. You yell that you are not appreciated, you do enough work already, your Mom wasn't there to pick you up on time, that you are old enough, that you are responsible enough, or everyone else is doing whatever it is that you aren't or can't do. Whatever you are yelling about, it won't work for you. In arguments or when you are not getting your way, the best thing to do is to <u>talk</u> to your parents. State clearly what you want and why you think you should be able to do it. Even if your parents are yelling at you, staying perfectly calm and talking to them will make them feel very immature for yelling at you. The lack of yelling also makes things easier when it comes time to forgive and forget.

Oh, yeah, if you are getting in trouble for something you did, be an adult and take responsibility for your actions. Yelling will almost always increase the length and severity of the punishment. Apologize. Explain the reasons why you did what you did and take the punishment. If you do this really authentically, usually the punishment will be lessened in the following day or so.

13) Don't pretend your parents are stupid.

Your parents were teenagers once, too, and they do know what is going on in your life. They might not know how hard you party or what the most popular drug is, but they do know that teenagers drink, party, and lie. If (even though I do not recommend this) you are going to lie to your parents, don't be so stupid as to pretend that your parents don't know some of the stuff you are doing. Parents (especially mothers) have some sort of sick sixth sense when it comes to their kids. I swear, a lot of parents can tell we have done something bad just by looking at our faces. Plus, you never know what your parents have read in your garbage can or on your floor or what they have found in dirty clothes on the way to the wash—not to mention that helpful telephone call they may have received from a friend's mother or father.

14) Apologize and "fess" up.

As I said earlier, the whole idea of apologizing when you are wrong is very important. If you did something bad, and you are getting punished, even if you think the punishment is unfair, you should apologize. If the whole story hasn't come out yet, you can set it right from the beginning, just in case some friend's mother does decide to call and give the details.

15) Say THANK YOU.

It might seem simple, but you have no idea how little we as teenagers say thank you to our parents. By showing your appreciation and showing your parents that you recognize all that they do for you, you can really improve your relationship with them. So many of the parents I talked to complained of feeling that their teenagers did not understand how lucky they were and how hard the parents worked for their money to give their kids the lifestyle and opportunities that they got. Saying thank you after your Mom cooks your dinner, after you go on a vacation, or even after your Dad drops you off at a party can make all the difference. Not only does it make our parents feel more appreciated for all that they do for us, but it also allows us honestly to be more thankful for how lucky we really are.

<u>Overview List for Teenagers</u>

How to Improve Your Relationship with Your Parents.
(This list can be torn out and put on a fridge or in the car or wallet.)

• Make a future plan.

• Know the college process.

• Check out all of your options.

• Keep notes.

• Get organized.

• Get homework binder.

• Tell your parents what is going on.

• Ask your parents what is going on.

• Act the way you want your parents to treat you.

• Be honest.

• Do extra for your parents.

• Don't blow up at your parents.

• Don't pretend your parents are stupid.

• Apologize.

• Say thank you.

PART III
What Parents Fear

"I am afraid that my teenager will one day grow up."
-Mother on what she was most afraid of for her thirteen-year-old daughter, 42

This section stands alone, because some of it is very blunt, very shocking, and very honest. In this section I talk about drugs, alcohol, sex, discrimination, the Internet, and other things that threaten teenagers and plague the minds of parents as they wait for their teenagers to come home at night. I hope this section will allow parents to better understand their teenagers, remember their own experiences, and see how they can help their teenagers face some pretty significant and scary issues. I believe if a parent knows what threatens their teens, the parent can talk to the teen about it and help provide coping skills which will reduce the threat of the dangers in the lives of teens. For teenagers, I hope you can read this section and realize you are not alone with what you experience and that you will hear and listen to this advice about how to deal with parents when it comes to things they don't want you to do.

The Truth about Drugs and Alcohol

"Everyone does it"
  -Response from a female, 16, when asked about the prevalence of drugs

"My daughter doesn't do it."
  -A father's response about how he thinks drugs affect his daughter

If you think your teenager hasn't had the opportunity to try drugs, you are probably wrong. Okay, let me clarify. The amount of drugs around each teenager depends on where they live, how old they are, and who they hang out with. But, unfortunately, drugs are everywhere.

I do not do drugs, but I have lots of friends who do drugs. I am frequently surrounded by them and often offered to smoke/sniff/injest. In the next couple of pages I will describe the teenage drug culture EVERY teenager is in whether they do drugs or not. I will also describe how teenagers have ruined their lives and their brains smoking too much pot, doing too much acid, or becoming alcoholics by the age of 15. One of the most frequent questions adults of all ages have asked me and other teenagers with whom they are close is, "What is the drug scene like today?" I realized, while writing this book and talking to adults about the drugs of their time and what they think their teenagers are doing, that the drug culture really does change with each generation. I had parents ask me about the popularity of Quaaludes. I had never heard of them. And I, on the other hand, have told parents about the popularity of Hashish. They had never heard of it.

Despite the huge variety of drugs available to teenagers today—and many are too easily accessible—there are still some drugs that are the more popular drugs than others. In fact, some of these drugs are so popular they are not even considered such bad drugs anymore. The biggest and most popular examples of this desensitization are marijuana and alcohol.

Marijuana

Weed, grass, bulls, joints, pot, tokey, junk, and more—marijuana is a huge part of teenage culture. Even if teenagers aren't doing marijuana themselves, they definitely know someone who is. There was always (according to most adults) "that group" in school and "those parties" that were known for having pot. Yet, for many more teens nowadays, pot is a part of daily social life and weekend fun.

Pot is definitely the most popular drug out there among teenagers. In fact, many teenagers despise smoking cigarettes, but have nothing against smoking pot. Why? Their argument is that cigarettes affect your appearance more drastically and your smell. Yellow teeth, dirty nails, smelly hair, smelly breath, raspy voice all come in a pack of cigarettes, while pot just "gives you a nice buzz" and is easily covered up with some cologne or breath mints—at least that is what some teenagers think.

Pot is also becoming more and more accessible because there are teenage drug dealers in every public and private high school in the nation. At the same time, anyone (teenager or not) can go down to a street corner or club in the bad part of town at night and buy "pot". I put "pot" in quotes because many of the street drug dealers today dilute their marijuana, or even worse, lace it with rat poison and/or LSD (not uncommon). The price of pot is also decreasing. On a teenager's tight budget, and with friends who are willing to sell, marijuana is much more appealing than a night at the movies or cigarettes.

There is something very important for teenagers and parents to understand. Most people, adults especially, think of people who use drugs or are druggies as the boy down the street with baggy pants, a bad smell, and unbrushed hair with a bad attitude. This is simply not true. I know that some of the smartest girls at my school smoke pot or do other more serious drugs. I have seen teenage Goths and football jocks smoke out together at a club or party. People have to understand that not only is marijuana considered somewhat of a soft drug, but also many people who you "would never expect" do it. Many adults think that they can tell if their teenager or his or her friends are doing drugs because of the parental sixth sense. The stereotypical druggie is no longer applicable, and parents often cannot detect this usage

Drug dealers are also not what most people would assume. Many times, teenage drug dealers are the smarter, entrepreneurial teenagers because they just want some extra cash. They have figured out how cheap pot can be, where to get it, where to sell it, and how huge the demand is. Some drug dealers that I know don't even smoke their own merchandise.

Right now it is also very cool to have good pot smoking equipment. Many of my teenage friends own bongs, pipes, and all kinds of rolling paper. Some of the bongs and pipes I have seen are actually quite beautiful with colored hand blown glass and all. Taking bongs hits together, passing the joint around a circle at a party, or sharing a pipe smoking session is not uncommon teenage behavior. This goes on at parties and concerts, on school lunch breaks, and in a teen's own bedroom.

Another example of the pot smoking culture for teens is one of the pot delivery systems in New York. Many of my friends who live in New York will call a number, and the operator will ask how much pot they want, what kind they want (there are different strands with varying properties and potencies), and where they want it delivered. Then, in usually two hours or less, a "delivery guy" will come to your teenager's house or wherever the teenager's delivery was agreed to occur and drop off the merchandise for a fee. This is how a lot of my friends in New York City get their marijuana. It is delivered to Park Avenue apartments, houses in Long Island, and apartments in Queens.

Alcohol

At teenage parties you usually smoke pot, drink beer, or go home. Alcohol is another one of the substances that is considered less harmful, lots of fun, and very cool, making it the other huge part of the teenage drug scene.

The first reason alcohol is so popular is that it is not illegal—entirely. If you have an older friend or parents who drink, or you get lucky with a very nice liquor store cashier, you can get a good amount of alcohol with a couple of bucks and a smile. The accessibility of alcohol, just like pot, is a major factor why it is so integral to teenage parties. Alcohol at a party is a necessity, and when I say necessity, I mean necessity. If there is talk of a party going around school on Thursday morning, the first question is, "Will there be parents home?" and the second question is, "How many kegs?" Many teenagers will not come to a party unless there is alcohol there, and they will not come if they need to bring their own booze.

The second reason alcohol is so popular is because it is not really considered a drug in typical teenager's minds. In fact, it is not considered anything serious at all. Even though alcoholism among teens is growing by the year, the effects of alcohol on the body and the mind are considered minimal, if not fun. People drink to lighten up at parties, be less nervous, and look cool, because everyone else is or because they like the taste.

Taste is the third reason why alcohol is so popular. It is one thing to cough when you smoke, or have your throat burn after you take a bong hit, but it is another to dislike the taste of alcohol—this is easily fixable. Alcohol, as we all know, comes in a variety of forms. Sex on the Beach, Cosmopolitans, Sunrises, Apple Martini's, and Rum with Coke are all fun to order and taste pretty good. For teenagers who don't like the taste of beer, whiskey or vodka, they can easily opt out for a sweeter drink that sounds cool, and with a fake ID at a club, these drinks can make you look pretty cool, too.

Just because the sweet, more "posh" drinks are becoming so popular, does not mean that the "harder" alcohol is going to die out. Far from it. What keeps hard liquor so popular is that this type of alcohol comes hand in hand with drinking games, machismo, and what is most likely in your parent's liquor cabinet. Drinking activities such as body shots, funneling, flip cup, beer pong, and shot races are popular ways for teenagers to spend Friday nights, especially when there are few or no underage activities in most cities and towns. The machismo thing is definitely thrown into the mix with alcoholic drinks because how much a man can "hold" and how much he can down in one night becomes a competition among many teenage guys. I have seen guys get in full-on fist fights after debating who can hold their liquor better. I have also seen guys drink themselves into alcohol poisoning and comas in a competition to see who could drink more during a vodka shot competition. When stubbornness and egos are combined with teenage drinking, it is no wonder we have so many teenage drinking accidents and trouble.

Lastly, many parents not only have lots of alcohol in their cabinets, but they also buy the alcohol for their teenagers. There are many parents who allow their teenagers to drink with them. I personally think that minimally allowing your teenagers a drink when they are around you is a good idea, because parents are able to regulate their kid's drinking and/or give their teenagers some leeway so that they don't explode and not know their own limits when they are drinking with friends. The problem arrives, however, when parents not only let their kids drink around them, but also when they buy their kids alcohol to drink during their free time as well as to give it away to their friends. Yet, I have had adults tell me, "Why shouldn't I buy the alcohol for them? If I don't, they will either steal it out of my cabinet or get it from some other illicit or illegal source." It is true that even when parents don't buy their kids and friends alcohol, the teenagers will almost always get it another way.

Hookah and Shrooms

Hashish is a type of tobacco with fruit in it. It is smoked out of bongs or water pipes, and it originated in Egypt. The little pieces of fruit or flavor give flavor to the smoke and a different type of experience to the smoker. In Los Angeles and in many other big cities, there are "Hashish bars" where 18-year-olds and up come and order a table and hashish and smoke over a cup of coffee or espresso. The problem is that many teenagers have fake IDs and attend the bars at their whim and for their fun. Again, not many teenagers believe that hookah tobacco is as bad as tobacco because it tastes much better.

Shrooms are definitely gaining momentum once again among teens. Shrooming with brownies or alone also seems less "hardcore" in most teenagers' minds. Fortunately, shrooms are more of a one-time experience for most teenagers rather than a habit or constant social accompaniment like marijuana or alcohol.

Prescription Drugs

The popularity of prescription drugs really depends on where you live and what kind of school you attend. In many private high schools across the nation, prescription drugs are a popular way to get high. Many students either sell drugs they have received from wisdom teeth operations and other pain traumas, or they save them and take the drugs themselves after they have already recovered for a different kind of high. Valium and Vicadin are two particularly popular prescription drugs. Teenagers can also steal anti-depressants or stimulant prescription pills from parents' medicine cabinets. Many of these pills are similar to Opiates and act as neurotransmitters in the nervous system. The prescription painkillers act as neurotransmitters and block nervous impulses from traveling through the nervous system and into the brain. Because the brain does not receive the nerve impulses (these can be anything from a light touch to a kick in the face), the body goes into a relaxed state. Sometimes the pressure in a teenager's life drives teenagers to crave and become addicted to this kind of numbness.

One of the most popular drugs out there in the teen kingdom today is Adderall. This is a frightening, yet ever popular, trend. Kids who have been diagnosed with ADD as a child or have siblings or friends who are prescribed Adderall are now taking it for recreation. Adderall is not used for parties, but is used to study all night. When a person who does not have ADD takes Adderall, it makes them hyperactive, and supposedly, able to retain more information. I would say about 40% of all students during final exam time in high school take Adderall to pull all nighters. I would say that percentage is more than 50% in most colleges and universities.

Many students will pass Adderall around during finals and think it is nothing more than a caffeine pill to help them study. You need to help your kids realize that Adderall is not similar to an over-the-counter caffeine pill. Teenagers themselves must understand the severe side effects of taking prescription drugs without a prescription to study or for recreation. Some of the more severe side effects of Adderall are heart palpitations, tachycardia, elevation of blood pressure and sudden death. Taking Adderall often also results in over stimulation, restlessness, dizziness, insomnia, euphoria, dyskinesia, dysphoria, depression, tremor, headaches, Tourette's syndrome, seizures and stroke. Some more physical side-effects are dryness of the mouth, unpleasant taste, diarrhea, constipation, other gastrointestinal disturbances as well as impotence and changes in libido.[1]

The Big Ones

There are definitely drugs that are considered more "hardcore" and are more rare amongst teenagers. They are not as popular, because they are more expensive, harder to find, have longer effects, and the effects are harder to hide from parents. Unfortunately, even though they are not the most popular, there is still widespread use of these serious drugs. *Ecstasy* has become a lot more popular with the influx of raves. Raves are huge parties where a large venue is rented out, people pay to get in, listen to techno music, dance, and most or all do ecstasy, or "E". Because this generation of teenagers is so into the techno and light stick craze, ecstasy has also become very appealing. The hook with ecstasy is that it arouses pleasure responses, and, therefore, it makes giant orgies another huge part of raves.

Cocaine and crystal methane have some popularity, despite the difficulty with obtaining them, because of their stimulant effect. As I have talked about earlier, the pressure to be skinny and do well in school is tremendous. Crystal methane can help you out with both of these things. Many girls and boys have begun to take these drugs because they get rid of your appetite, give you more energy, increase your metabolism so you burn off weight, and allow you to stay up all night cramming for tests. It is horrible on your body, but worth it for too many teenagers today. I had a friend who was taking crystal methane five times a day for a couple of months, and no one could tell because it is so easy to hide.

---

1.   July 18, 2006. <www.webmd.com>

Heroin and LSD, or Acid, are not as popular with teens, because they are very expensive.

Over-the-Counter Drugs and Odd Substitutions

This phenomenon always disturbed me because of the carefree attitude that seems to go along with doing these kinds of drugs and drug substitutions. First, many teenagers are addicted to over-the-counter drugs of all kinds. Teens take sleeping pills so that they can go to sleep when they get in bed without having to stress so much about their lives. They take pain killers because the pressure on high school athletes is so high that if they take the pain killers, they can keep performing in their sport despite injuries. And there are, of course, the teenagers who drink lots of cough syrup to get a supposed wicked high.

I know many of these addictions and obsessions with over-the-counter drugs sound odd, but these substances are used because they are easy to get and cheap—two things that are definitely on a teenager's priority list. I think some of the drug substitutions are even more worrisome than the over-the-counter drugs. These drug substitutions include whiteout, markers, aerosol cans, paint, and glue. I have seen boys go to the bathroom at a dance and start sniffing permanent markers to get a buzz. It is easy enough to buy school supplies, even though sniffing or "puffing" usually gives you more of a headache than a high.

Steroids

Steroids are (luckily) not as popular today as they have been with other generations. Part of the reason is that athletes are being drug tested more frequently. Additionally, steroids are harder to obtain today. You might be wondering how so many athletes in school do drugs—because many do. This is very disturbing, but unfortunately, very true. In many high schools, teenagers are being drug tested if they are on sports teams, and some are even randomly tested even if they have no sports affiliation. How is it that so many athletes are showing up "clean" after a weekend of fun, drinking, and smoking? The answer is urine dealers. Yes, that's right. Teenagers are selling "clean pee" to athletes who need to be drug tested. I know many buyers and a couple of dealers in this business, and this is a pretty popular way to pass the drug testing. One says, "I get my little brothers to pee in cups and then sell the shit for like 20 bucks a pop. If I have to make a delivery, I charge 30 bucks for a jar of urine. It's pretty profitable." Scary, yes; filthy, yes; unheard of, no.

In a typical weekend, you might be wondering, how is the drug scene played out? Usually parties are planned at the houses where parents aren't home, kegs are bought, and pot is stashed. Usually the drug and alcohol stay at the weekend parties or teenagers do it in the car before a concert or in the back yard of someone's house on a Saturday night. Then they go to see a "really trippy movie". Mostly the drug scene for teenagers is a weekend habit. Another problem is that the drug use does sometimes leak over into the week. The use doesn't become an "every other weekend thing" but a weekly, daily, hourly addiction. Teenagers who don't take school seriously or have lots of extra time on their hands will end up smoking pot on lunch breaks at school in the bathroom. Eventually, a fun thing that was done with friends turns into a "when I wake-up, before I go to bed habit … kind of like brushing your teeth." Scary, but true.

STATS AND FACTS (FROM HTTP://WWW.GDCADA.ORG/INDEX.HTM)

- Data from the National Household Survey on Drug Abuse reveals that almost 3 million adolescents and about seven million young adults from ages 18–25 have used prescription drugs for non-medical purposes at least once in their lives. That number caps a steady increase beginning with the mid-1980s. Increases in prescription drug abuse is most prominent for pain relievers, but use of stimulants and tranquilizers is also rising.

- An estimated 2.3 million kids ages 12-17 abused legal medications last year, according to the Center on Addiction and Substance Abuse at Columbia University.

- Teenagers whose parents talk to them regularly about the dangers of drugs are 42% less likely to use drugs than those whose parents don't, yet only 1 in 4 teens reports having these conversations.[1]

- Alcohol is the most commonly used drug among young people.[2]

- Alcohol kills 6½ times more youth than all other illicit drugs combined.[2]

- Youth who drink alcohol are 50 times more likely to use cocaine than young people who never drink alcohol.[2]

- 40% of those who started drinking at age 14 or younger later developed alcohol dependence compared with 10% of those who began drinking at age 20 or older.[2]

- 65% of the youth who drink alcohol report that they get the alcohol they drink from family and friends.[2]

- 10% of teens say that they have been to a rave, and ecstasy was available at more than two-thirds of these raves.[3]

- Although it is illegal to sell and distribute tobacco products to youth under age 18, most underage smokers are able to buy tobacco products.[2]

- Underage drinking costs the U.S. more than $58 billion every year—enough to buy every public school student a state-of-the-art computer.[4]

- 28% of teens know a friend or classmate who has used ecstasy with 17% knowing more than one user.[3]

- By the 8th grade, 52% of adolescents have consumed alcohol, 41% have smoked cigarettes, and 20% have used marijuana.[2]

- In 2000, more than 60% of teens said drugs were used, kept, or sold at their school.[3]

- 50% of high school seniors report drinking alcohol in the past 30 days with 32% reporting being drunk at least once in the same period.[2]

- Most people begin smoking as adolescents. Among youths who smoke, the average age of initiation is 12.5 years of age.[2]

- Drivers age 21–29 drive the greatest proportion of their miles drunk. (Miller et al., 1996c)

- Traffic crashes are the greatest single cause of death for all persons age 6–33. About 45% of these fatalities are alcohol-related crashes.[2]

[1] Partnership For A Drug-Free America
[2] Substance Abuse: *The Nation's Number One Health Problem*
[3] National Survey of Substance Abuse Attitudes, Feb. 2001
[4] Mothers Against Drunk Driving

This section was neither meant to put parents reading these statistics in shock, nor is the intention to induce a deep stage or paranoia about their own teenager. I also hope that I don't have teenagers knocking at my door, up in arms, saying that I told too much. Now is the part where I give advice, reasons, and the possible silver lining to the teenage drug situation.

Why are We Doing Drugs?

After speaking with hundreds of teenagers about drugs and the drug scene over the past eight teenage years of my life, I can tell you that the biggest reason why teenagers do drugs is usually overlooked by most adults. **Boredom**. In so many cities and towns all over the nation, teenagers have nothing to do on Friday and Saturday nights. To get a thrill and to forget about how bored they are, they drink, smoke, and get into trouble. Underage clubs are rare and expensive. You can only see a movie so many times. Staying home with the family and watching TV is not always the coolest thing to do. The biggest reason that teenagers are doing drugs is not really to escape from reality, loosen up, or have fun. The reason is that there is really nothing better to do. A 16-year-old friend of mine says, "It is much better to be bored and drunk than just bored." And for many it is just the thrill of buying some alcohol or weed that breaks the boredom. Of course, the drinking and smoking happens because the drugs are there.

Drugs are a recreational activity and source of amusement for many teens. But teens also say they use drugs, because "it allows them to loosen up and they like the feeling." Many teenage guys are finally able to hit on a girl when they are drinking, or not be so self conscious when they have a beer, or they finally stop worrying about school when they have a joint. The general difference in behavior is attractive to most teenagers because of the growing self-consciousness that happens in the teenage years.

Peer pressure is also a factor. If everyone is doing it around you and they don't think it is a big deal, why should you? Many teenagers get started smoking and drinking because everyone else is doing it.

How to Prevent Drug Problems with Your Teenagers

I look at the way that other teenagers and I, who do not do drugs, have been brought up and at their reasons for not participating in the drug scene that surrounds teenagers parties, lives, and actions, and I see one common theme. **My parents talked to me openly and honestly about drugs starting at a very young age.** They were informative and clear, not threatening and condescending. Here are some ways that parents can **alienate their teenagers** when it comes to doing drugs. <u>DO NOT DO THE FOLLOWING:</u>

- <u>Do not keep silent</u>. Never bringing up the looming threat of drugs at younger and younger ages is something that might seem like the easy way out, but it is actually really dangerous. Many parents think that their kids are too young to talk about doing serious drugs at parties or socially with friends. Well, you might think they are too young, but the average age at school where drugs begin to become an issue (entering in conversations, friends of friends who are doing pot on the weekend) is the ripe age of 10. That is correct. Many fifth and sixth graders are beginning to face questions about staying clean or being cool. So not talking about drugs to your kids or waiting until it is too late can make your kids believe what their friends are saying instead of what you could tell them. These rumors can be as dangerous as "marijuana is not addictive" to "shooting cocaine does less damage than sniffing it."

- <u>Do not be too authoritative</u> when having the drug talk. You can give your kids the best pamphlets and most informative drug talk in the world and alienate your kids even more. Unfortunately, teenagers have a tendency to do "bad things" just because their parents said not to or just to piss their parents off. Drugs play an important role in these kinds of situations. Parents' intentions definitely play a part in how much and when teenagers do drugs. Sometimes it is to get back at parents and assert independence. Other times it is to forget about the constant pressure parents can put on their teenagers to do work, be smart, and go to a good college. If a parent is too authoritative when giving the drug talk, a teenager can be turned off. "Too authoritative" is when a parent threatens a teenager by talking about the "horrible trouble you will get into if you ever touch alcohol or drugs," or "you will never be the same after you do drugs, so don't ever try drugs or you will be sorry." Mostly, your teenagers know that you were once teenagers as well, and that you have probably tried and experimented yourself, so threats and condescending remarks such as, "I know about these things, don't try any drugs," make us not trust you. Be honest and open when talking to your teenager and hear their perspective on drugs. **Have a discussion not a lecture.**

- <u>Do not restrict your teen too much</u>. I point out that one of the major causes of drug usage is boredom. So, one of the best things you can do to keep your kids out of drugs is to give them other fun options of things to do. Take them to bowling alleys, let them go see movies, take them on camping trips, encourage weekend sports games and tournaments with your teen and their friends. Have barbecues at your house where you are there and can organize food and music. Even in large cities like Los Angeles and New York, there are very few under-age things to do. Research underage places for your kids. Take them, or better yet, drop them off at a live concert for underage kids. However, you need to make sure to drop them off and pick them up so you know what they are doing. Encouraging sports and teams, community service, and other physical activities is the best way to keep your kids away from drugs, because anything physical keeps them busy, gives them reason not to smoke, and allows them to meet other kids with similar interests.

The best thing to do when talking to teenagers about drugs is to be honest, especially if you yourself have tried drugs. Talk not only about the consequences, but also the importance of experimenting. I know I probably am losing a lot of parents right about now, but I believe that a huge reason why my brother, friends, and I do not do drugs is because our parents offered to smoke our first cigarette with us, give us our first drink under their supervision, and encouraged us to talk to them about what drugs we were interested in discussing. Here is a huge concept and tip in dealing with teenagers because of our mentality and culture:

The more you restrict and hold your teenager back, the more they will want to explode when outside of your supervision.

Please don't get me wrong here. I am not saying to let your teenager do whatever drugs, sex, and rock and roll they want. I am saying this: **If you give your teenager trust and leeway, your teenager will not feel the need to rebel.**

The Impact of Health Class

You might be wondering what teenagers learn from health class, and if health class helps teenager's views on drugs. To be honest, most teenagers consider health class a joke. If anything, a lot of teenagers find the 80's videos quite amusing and funny. This does not mean that health classes are worthless, however they just do not do much in shaping teenager's opinions. One problem is that in most schools, health class comes too late. Leaving out the videos and lectures on teenage sexuality (to come later), the information and "introduction" to drugs is too late, because young teenagers have already heard, or possibly even done, a lot of the drugs that the teacher talks about in class. The second reason for the diminishing impact of health class is the fact that the class is usually taught by a female teacher in her sixties talking about something from which she is most likely very removed in the real world. It is hard for a teenager to absorb or relate to anything in this type of situation.

The one impact that health class does have is the informational aspect. Rumors and myths fly in the fifth and six grades, especially about drugs and sex. When my sister was in fourth grade, we were all sitting at the dinner table. My brother and I were in the tenth and eleventh grades at the time, and she asked us both if we had smoked "the pot".

"You know," she said, "like in the kitchen … I think."

My Dad quickly changed the subject, and we all continued eating. The first disturbing thing about this somewhat comical situation was that she had heard people talking about "the pot". She had no idea, however, that was marijuana, and so she asked us about it. She thought it was kitchen equipment! This is where health class can be very helpful. Health class is a good way of stomping out myths among young teens and clarifying what is addictive and what isn't.

The class is also good for young teens to see the consequences of some of the drugs they might have heard about from friends. The program "D.A.R.E" has policemen go to schools and talk about the different drugs and what kind of trouble people can get into by taking them. This program is great, and I still remember the officer who came to my school once a week for ten weeks to speak. He had a big effect on how I think about the legal consequences of doing drugs.

People Do Get into Trouble

While it is obvious for most parents, a lot of teens don't realize the huge impact that drugs can have on a person's health and future. Here are three stories:

#1—An old friend of mine named *Steve used to be one of the best guys. He went to my break dancing class with me, and he was the best dancer in the class. He was also an amazing looking guy who was always well dressed, tanned, and extremely courteous. That's right. He seemed to get anything he wanted. He was the funniest and nicest guy I had ever met. He had a really quick wit and did pretty well in school, but he was usually focused on dancing and hanging out with friends. We often went to parties and dances on the weekend to do routines together and meet new people. This was in ninth grade. He and I were both 14 years old. In January of freshman year he started to smoke a little marijuana after we finished dancing. Then he started smoking before dance class to "loosen up". He started doing shrooms, and he was always high. It didn't really affect his dancing, but it did affect his already average schoolwork. This is when he decided to start taking crystal methane. When I asked him why, he said, "It is a great idea. I mean, it will give me energy so our routines are really kick-ass, and then I will be able to stay up all night studying instead of getting tired so that I can get my school work up." Doing crystal meth a few times a month turned to every day then five times a day and then into doing cocaine.

It took a year for Steve's drug habit to progress to this stage. When he started doing crystal meth more than twice a week, I stopped dancing with him. In fact, he stopped dancing all together, and he stopped studying all together. He stayed home, got high, and watched TV. I hadn't seen him for nine months, and then I saw him at a party.

I didn't even realize it was him until his friend came over and said, "Hey, long time no see!"

"Hey, Brett" I said, "How are you? How is Steve?"

"What are you talking about?" he said, "Steve is right over there. Didn't you see him?"

Well, I hadn't seen him. In fact, you could barely see him. He was so skinny you could see his bones through his shirt. His skin was yellow, and his eyes were sunken in with dark circles around them. I went over to him. He was sitting by himself, and he said, "Hey." He was really happy to see me, I think. I couldn't really understand him because he was having trouble speaking. I asked him questions, but he only answered with, "It's cool." He had stopped dancing and doing everything except getting high and taking hits. I left the party soon after that and heard two months later that he was in a special hospital because he couldn't do normal daily functions anymore. According to his parents, he was "too fried for the real world".

#2—A pretty crazy and wild girlfriend of mine named *Maggie always liked to party. She started smoking and drinking at age 12 in seventh 7th grade. She always assured me and everyone else that she just did it at parties, that she was always careful, and that she only did it around people she knew. In ninth grade she started to party all the time with her older friends. Doing drugs is a pretty expensive habit, and she was running out of allowance really quickly. She started stealing money from her parents, from her teachers, and from random people. She would do this after she got high to give her, if I remember correctly, "… a big rush and quick hands." Despite her drug use, Maggie actually had pretty good grades and played the flute really well. She was able to keep her grades up despite nightly parties. She planned to go to college and become a music teacher or "something educationally artsy" as she used to say. After a couple of months of stealing to support her habit, her hands were obviously not quick enough, because she got caught, arrested, drug tested, and put in juvenile hall. All of her plans for college were ruined. She had to stop playing the flute because she was in rehab. Her parents had no idea what she had been doing, because her grades were still good. She had just seemed distant to them.

#3—Last, a much less extreme story, but nonetheless devastating. A friend of mine smoked pot on the weekend. He never sold drugs, and he kept his pipe and some baggies in the car for the times he went out on the weekends. He was neither a serious smoker nor was he addicted. One day as he was driving into school, school security and police officers were checking cars for drugs and weapons. He got stopped, and his car was searched. Even though he was not a drug dealer, addicted. or even a heavy smoker, his pipe and baggies were labeled as "drug dealer paraphernalia", and he was arrested. Another kid at school who didn't particularly like him told the cops during an interview that my friend who had gotten arrested had sold him pot. My friend is now in juvenile hall doing time for one year, and he will have 100 hours of community service plus a year of school to make up and no college plans when he gets back. You don't have to be a drug dealer, a serious druggie, or even doing drugs to be caught and have your future taken away. If you are in a car with others doing drugs or caught with one joint on you, you can be arrested.

These are only three examples of things that can happen to people if they get involved with drugs. There are so many other people who have better and worse endings to similar stories. Many teens try drugs eventually. My best advice is that if you decide to make that choice, do it safely and responsibly with the consequences known and in mind.

*all names have been changed

Sex and Teenagers

"I mean, I respect my body, I am not stupid enough not to protect myself, but I think I am ready to have sex."
  -Female, 16

"I want her to have a healthy sex life when she is 34."
  -Father, 48, on when his daughter should be able to have sex.

Desensitization

In my opinion desensitization is the word that characterizes the mindset most teenagers have when it comes to sex. We see it everywhere—in movies, the Internet, on TV, and at school. The standards for what is appropriate and acceptable have lowered significantly in the past couple of years. Some examples:

1. If you turn on MTV and watch just three of the videos shown, you are guaranteed to see at least one thong, two people making out with heavy petting, or a young girl in next to nothing shaking what Momma gave her.

2. At the movie theater, PG-13 movies are allowed to show breasts and/or mild, but nevertheless obvious sex scenes.

3. Regular after school or early evening television programs tackle the sex issues and are brought up with strong innuendos, scantily dressed girls, and vocabulary such as "blow job," "going down," and "hooking up."

    By pointing these things out, I am not at all suggesting that parents should forbid their teenagers from watching MTV or going to anything but PG movies. I think what is important is to point out that sex is more readily available, less taboo. and more popular than it has ever been. As I will go on to discuss, other forms of sexual activity are as well.

    This desensitization has done three things. The first is it has "educated" younger teens and kids about sex. At younger and younger ages more kids are learning about sex and in the wrong ways. The second effect is teenagers are less sensitive about what sex really means. The importance and sacredness of being close with another person has been lost. The third effect of desensitization is, as was stated before, kids are learning about sex, but learning incorrectly. If you notice, almost never in a love scene in a movie or on a TV show do you see the couple using any sort of protection or contraceptive. You almost always just see the act itself. So, by only seeing this and not talking to parents or having classes at school, teens and kids can get dangerously misleading presumptions and information.

Parents cannot stop or prevent their teenagers and kids from experiencing the huge amount of sexual openness expressed in the media. They can't stop kids at school from talking about sex even if they do succeed in sheltering their child. I think sheltering a young teen from what other teenagers are inevitably learning about can be more harmful than helpful. As was mentioned in a previous chapter: **The more parents hold their teenagers back, the more they we will want to explode later.**

Even though parents cannot prevent their kids from learning about sex, they can talk to them about it so they understand what they are seeing. As discussed in the drug chapter, the impact of health class can be minimal. Kids who are in sixth to ninth grades (the usual time for health classes) are usually too uncomfortable with the topic around their friends to absorb much of the information given to them on sexually transmitted diseases and other forms of protection.

Many parents I talked to in formulating this book expressed the dread and anxiety that comes with giving their kids "the talk". Similarly enough, many teenagers joke about their first talk and how they dread getting it before any party. I asked parents and teenagers what could be done to make "the talk" less painful and more helpful. Here are the findings.

The Talk

For parents:

- Know what you are talking about. Make sure to know about the facts of life and any new forms of contraceptives that are out there.

- Don't assume your teenager or child already knows what certain things are and what you do with them. They might think they know, and they could be very wrong.

- Be willing to answer questions … any questions. If your child is old enough to get the talk, then the answer, "You will know when you are older," will not suffice. Coming to terms with your kids as sexually active beings is hard, but it is going to happen, and probably sooner than you expect.

- Short and to the point. Stories about your own childhood or beating around the bush make it more miserable for the both of you.

- If you are going to have the talk, then have the entire talk. Do not plan on talking about sexual intercourse this year and oral sex next year. Have it once. A huge mistake is giving the talk in many different ways over your child's teenage years, especially before they are going on their first date, are on their way to a party, or have just watched a sexual movie. Those are never opportune times.

- Point out the emotional side to sex. I think that a lot of teenagers today treat sex solely as a pleasure-seeking activity. It is important for parents to explain the difference between having sex and making love.

  Eventually, your kids are going to become sexually active. It is not uncommon or unnecessary for dads to buy their teenage boys condoms or for moms to ask their teenage daughters if they want to go on the pill. For many parents I talked to, this seemed an impossibility. All I had to say was, "Think about it. Would you rather give your daughter birth control or worry what to do when she gets pregnant?"

For Teenagers:

- Hopefully, by the time you have hit 13 your parents have given you the talk, but if not, listen. DO NOT act like you already know everything your parents are saying. First, this might scare them. Second, it is disrespectful. Third, you probably don't know it all anyway. Listening without rolling your eyes, putting your hands over your ears (which is tempting), or interrupting it what will make it go faster and easier on your parents and on you.

- No matter how uncomfortable you are, your parents are probably even more uncomfortable. They are not only realizing that their kids are growing up, but they also have to come to terms with their kids doing what THEY did as teenagers.

- Feel free to ask questions. If you are curious, ask. Your parents are safe, and they do know what they are talking about on these issues.

To be brutally honest, if your teenager wants to have sex, they will.

Before I bring this section to a close, I want to stress the fact that no matter how hard parents try to restrict their kid's sexuality, teenagers will find a way. Whether it is actually having sex, watching porn, or having a girlfriend, the teenage years are a time of experimentation. All parents remember how hormones affect the minds of teenage boys and how peer pressure invades the minds of teenage girls.

When dealing with your teenager and sex, the best policy is to be open and honest. Your kids are going to experiment with your consent or without it.

Many parents asked me, "How open should I be with my kids when having the talk? In my experience there are a few different ways to handle it. I picked three different cases from my friends and contacts, each exemplifying different approaches.

Case 1: The Do Nothing Talk

Unfortunately, this is probably the most common approach that I have heard in my interviews and among my friends.

The approach: These parents are nervous or uncomfortable even with the thought of saying words like penis, vagina, insertion, orgasm, or ejaculation in front of their kids. First, the kids are too young. The parents avoid PG-13 movies and even change the channel when sex scenes come on TV. As the kids get older and turn into tweens and young teenagers, the parents realize that their children might be approaching the age for the talk, but the parents assume that health class will explain birth control and how sex works.

The outcome: These kids will learn about sex on the playground, from friends, and from what they see on TV after parents go to bed. As I have explained before, health class comes too late and does not explain about the importance of an emotional connection that comes with sex. Unfortunately, kids do see a lot of sex in movies and on TV. They begin to hear on the playground all sorts of misconceptions about sex and blow jobs. One of my friends who never had the talk from her parents thought that pulling out (the man takes his penis out of the vagina right before he ejaculates) was a perfectly safe form of birth control. Her parents had neither explained that lubrication from the man released into the vagina contains sperm and can cause pregnancy, nor had the parents emphasized the dangers of STDs.

Please, please, please talk to your kids about sex, love, and STDs. Otherwise, they might hear the real information too late or not at all. Also, if you avoid discussing sex all together, your teenager might grow up thinking that sex is wrong.

It is important to explain to your teenager that it is perfectly natural to have sexual feelings and that they should not be ashamed of those feelings. If parents allow teenagers to grow up thinking that sex is taboo, they will not develop healthy relationships with their own lovers or spouses.

Case 2: The Self-Conscious Talk

The approach: These parents tackle the talk however awkward and scary it might be. They explain to their kids about STDs, loving your sexual partner, and that sex is okay with someone you care about if you do it responsibly.

The outcome: These kids understand what a healthy relationship is. They might still take risks or do stupid things, but a girl who has had an explanatory talk from her parents will not believe it when a guy tells her that she cannot get an STD if she is a virgin. These teenagers grow up knowing that sex can be a healthy and wonderful part of life.

Case 3: The Abundant Information Talk

The approach: A bit more rare, but nonetheless successful, these parents want their teenagers to embrace sexuality when they are ready and be responsible and well-informed lovers. They buy their kids technique books, books on the art of lovemaking, or Kama Sutra books that explain the importance and joy of orgasms and sexual healing. These parents do not encourage unprotected or wild sex, but they do want their kids to understand the importance of a healthy sex life and want them to be good lovers in the future.

The outcome: As opposed to what many parents would think, these kids actually are less sexually explorative than their peers. Because they know about sex and feel good about it, they do not use sex as a means to rebel. Whereas kids in the "parents do not have the talk category" feel sex is "wrong" or that it should be kept a secret, truly informed teens feel comfortable about sex and sexual situations. Teens who sneak out in the middle of the night to have unprotected sex because they do not know the importance of protection or the real significance of sexual intimacy suffer into adulthood.

A Thing or Two About Oral Sex

"A blow job is a blow job, its not sex, I am still a virgin and you can't get any diseases from it."

-Female when asked about the difference between oral sex and sex, 15
(And yes, I corrected her that you can get STD's from oral sex.)

When it comes to sex, this generation of teenagers has been bombarded with safe sex messages. In almost any teen magazine you open I guarantee that you can see at least two safe sex advertisements or articles promoting condoms, abstinence, and the dangers of sexually transmitted diseases. The good thing is, we got it. Safe sex and fear of STDs is definitely a part of any sexually active teenager's life. Many of the teenagers I interviewed would never even think of having sex without a condom *and* being on the pill. Many teenagers who are having sex either with a serious boyfriend or girlfriend or not are using condoms the way their parents lectured them and are being careful about STDs and AIDS. Unfortunately, while safe sex and abstinence are being advertised and included in the sex talks, oral sex is not.

Many parents will give the sex talk without even mentioning the dangers or significance of oral sex. You see commercials stating, "No glove, no love." This message is important, but so is the safe oral sex message. You might be wondering how much oral sex affects the lives of teenagers today.

Teenagers know it affects us a lot, because many young teenagers (13 and 14 years old) don't know the dangers of oral sex, that STDs can be contracted, or it is an act of love just as much as sexual intercourse and should not be taken lightly.

I interviewed and know many teenagers who believe that oral sex and blowjobs are not serious. Not meaning to scare parents, but there are too many girls who will meet a boy at a party and an hour later be giving a blowjob to the boy in the next room. As I said before, the reason for this is teenagers are not told about the dangers and significance of oral sex. Even though it can be quite uncomfortable, it is important for parents not only to let their kids know what oral sex is, but also to stress to them that it is just as important to wait for oral sex as it is to wait for sexual intercourse.

What Happens When We Don't Hear It from Our Parents?

Briefly it is important to share some things kids and young adults can believe if they are not given the sex talk early and honestly.

#1—A friend of mine named Kathy was sitting on the school bus in ninth grade (15 years old) listening to a bunch of the other girls in the bus talk about blowjobs. She had no idea what they were and asked the girls who were distant friends of hers. The girls laughed, and one of them decided to explain it. After the girl was done graphically describing it to get more of an effect, Kathy was very upset. She said, "My mom told me that was dirty so shouldn't you wash it first?" In this case Kathy's parents had obviously had the oral sex talk with Kathy, but not very honestly and had merely described oral sex as dirty, telling her that this part of a male's body is dirty. Kathy is still known as "the girl who thinks it's dirty."

#2—I don't know how many girls and boys have been made fun of for years, because until eighth grade they thought that a blow job was when you blow on the other person.

#3—This is a general statement because it applies to so many teenagers and people today: Girls are givers; boys are takers. For some reason, either because of the lack of parental advice, the media, or because it is what everyone else does, girls assume they are to please the boys in a relationship and that boys do not have to do anything. This assumption is carried on throughout adulthood and results in problematic sexual habits and relationships. If you don't believe you can have a talk with your son or daughter about the importance of pleasing your partner, then you have to imagine what your sex life would be like if it were one-sided. If they don't hear it from you, they might never realize it is important to be equal in a relationship with the opposite sex.

The "isms" and Phobias

"I would be really upset if my son brought home someone who wasn't our religion or color."

-Father on interracial dating and marriage

Racism, sexism, anti-Semitism, and homophobia cross all generations, all socio-economic levels, and all country borders. The hatred generated from these stereotypes and discrimination grows from the general ignorance of many people today. We live in a society of ignorance. It is ignorance that kills people, ideas, and cultures.

I wish I could say this generation of teenagers has overcome many racist and prejudiced ideas, but I cannot. Discrimination exists everywhere, and even though it has gotten better, it still is a part of teenagers' lives. This section is tricky because racism, sexism, homophobia, xenophobia, and anti-Semitism vary depending on the area lived in, the school the teenager attends, their family, their friends, and the race or gender of each and every teenager. I used to think our teenagers today prized tolerance as well as racial and sexual liberation. I thought that our generation of teenagers was not racist and instead intrigued by people different from them. But then I learned Los Angeles is different. I have lived in Los Angeles all my life. I went to a school with friends of all races and backgrounds. I am exposed to a huge variety of people and was raised in a family of Jews and Christians. I have been to Church and Temple with my family, and I have been taught the magnitude of open-mindedness. Many of my friends who are white try to be black and are humorously labeled "whiggers". In many aspects, it is cool to be accepted into every different racial group at school, to dress like an African American or dance like an Asian American. It is not uncommon to hear hardcore rap music and "gang slang" blaring right outside of Beverly Hills High School. In fact, you're cooler if you do this than if you don't.

When I began to travel around the country and the globe, I learned such tolerance and open-mindedness were unique to Los Angeles and other choice areas. I was shocked in my early teens when I heard my first racist joke and when I met people who supported the KKK and other anti-Semitic groups. Discrimination can be rampant and terrorizing in certain high schools across America. In fact, in certain areas teenagers have never met a Jewish person or a black person. Because they have never met people who are different and have never been taught different or similar ways and customs of other people's cultures, they assume certain stereotypes about them. This is why the isms and the phobias have not disappeared—ignorance. There is definitely more tolerance today than there ever was because of the education teenagers get through films, TV, and school, yet it is the ignorance of unknown people which keeps discrimination alive.

Many teenagers I met who were racist could not give me any reason for their prejudices. When asked, many didn't understand certain stereotypes aren't true, and that is why they were called stereotypes. It is also the lack of parental teaching which leads to ignorance and discrimination. Locke argued men are shaped and constructed by their environment. As humans, we are conditioned by what goes on around us. When we are little, our parents tell us what is right and wrong. Our friends and towns construct a moral reality that becomes real. Many parents who are prejudiced themselves pass their beliefs on to their kids. Several teenagers I know who have racist parents are still able to learn in school and from their own first hand experiences from being around people who are different. They learn that their parents' stereotypes were wrong. Others grow up with the same close-minded beliefs that their parents have. Still other times, parents who are not necessarily racist or discriminatory towards others do not instill a sense of open-mindedness in their kids.

Many teenagers who are homosexual have told me how afraid they were to tell their parents of their sexual orientation because of comments about other gay friends or actors. One friend who isn't gay had her mom tell her in a conversation about getting married, "I could never understand why you wouldn't want to get married, but I guess that isn't as bad as finding out you are gay." Many teenagers also are becoming more tolerant and participating in interracial and inter-religious dating. This normal and healthy issue becomes chastised and blurred when teenagers have to hide their significant others and even their friends who are other races because their parents will not allow it. These kinds of restrictions imposed by parents upon their teenagers are not uncommon today. It is these comments and limitations that debilitate future promises of peace and tolerant living.

In today's American society, we promote a cultural value system which stands for open opportunity and equality for all. It is crucial to teach your kids and teenagers the importance of acceptance and tolerance and to banish ignorant stereotypes in order to have a future world of peace.

The Internet

"I don't know what people did without the Internet, I talk to my friends, find new ones and surf for school."

-Boy, 13

"Maybe If I could understand the Internet, it wouldn't make me so nervous, the problem is my kids are on it all the time, and I have no idea who they can meet or what they can see."

-Mother, 39

Parents seem to think that by being on the Internet, teenagers are going to meet strangers, watch porn, and be completely influenced by the gambling and prescription drug ads that pop up. Honestly, it is really not a big deal.

Teenagers know the difference between talking to a stranger and talking to a friend. We know not to give out any personal information on the Internet in chat rooms and to stay away from NC-17 sites. All young adults need is to be told about these potential dangers once. Parents need to warn their kids when they first start using the Internet what the house rules are for using the Internet and that they must stay away from chat rooms and strangers if the kids are young.

A huge mistake many parents make is they overreact to the Internet. The Internet is a way teenagers socialize, exercise freedom, and explore. If anything, I think exploration of the Internet should be encouraged by parents. Many parents put parental controls on teen's computers and snoop in their kid's emails. This is a huge mistake! By snooping in kid's emails, reading IM's over their shoulders, or putting controls on what sites they can and cannot visit, you are basically telling your teenager you don't trust them and that they have no independence. The parental controls issues are important for younger adults and kids, but for teenagers over 13 it can cause rifts in the parent/teen relationship.

The more parents hold their teenagers back, the more they will want to explode later.

Your teenagers, especially teenage boys, are going to look at pornography. If they aren't looking on the Internet, then they'll look for it on TV, in magazines, or at a friend's house. It is normal, and even though most parents, especially mothers, find it disturbing, almost every teenage boy does it and will do it with parental controls there or not.

The privacy issue comes up a lot when it comes to the Internet. I have heard my friends and other teenagers talk about the countless times their parents begin to read their conversations with friends over their shoulder while on the Internet or go into their emails and read them when they are not home. By breaking into the personal privacy of your kids, you will not only make them hide more from you as parents, but you will also make them resent you. <u>No matter how much information you think you are finding out about your kids by reading their emails, you will know much less for a long time if they ever find out, because you will lose their trust.</u>

A note about MySpace, Facebook and Friendster

A lot of parents ask me about my opinion about kids putting up profiles on these sites. I think that as long as parents explain the dangers of stalkers, and they set up rules about chatting with strangers, these sites are a part of the teenage world today, and restricting your child or prohibiting them from joining will only make them resent you more.

How to Get Help

General Teen Help (any subject/crisis)

National Teen Emergency Hotline: 1-800-448-3000
National Teen Hotline: 1-800-234-8336
National Crisis Help Line: 1-800-233-4357

Abuse/Violence Child Protective Services: 1-810-412-6109
Family Violence Helpline: 1-800-996-6228
National Domestic Violence Hotline: 1-800-799-7233
National Referral Network for Kids In Crisis: 1-800-543-7283

Alcohol/Drugs

Alateen/Al-Anon for the friends/family of alcoholics: 1-800-813-3105 or 1-800-356-9996
Alcohol and Drug Helpline: 1-800-821-4357
National Council on Alcoholism & Drug Dependancy Hope Line: 1-800-622-2255
Marijuana Anonymous: 1-800-766-6779
American Council for Drug Education: 1-800-488-3784

Anorexia/Bulimia/Eating Disorders

Eating Disorders Information and Referral Line: 1-800-931-2237
National Crisis Line—Anorexia and Bulimia: 1-800-233-4357
Overeaters Abuse Hotline: 1-800-888-4680
National Eating Disorder Hotline: 1-800-248-3285
Food Addiction Hotline: 1-800-872-0088

Cancer

American Cancer Society: 1-800-ACS-2345
American Lung Association: 1-800-586-4872

Cutting—if you cut yourself

Hotline for Teens Who Cut: 1-800-366-8288

Depression/Grief/Loss of a Loved One

National Grief Recovery Help Line: 1-800-848-9595
National Depression Association: 1-800-826-3632

Divorce—Dealing with Your Parents' Divorce

Boys Town Hotline (for Girls AND Boys): 1-800-448-3000
Carezone Web Site—kids helping kids deal with divorce

Gay/Lesbian

Gay and Lesbian Hotline: 1-888-843-4564
National Hotline for Gay, Lesbian, Bi and Transgendered Youth: 1-800-347-8336
PRIDE Institute for Lesbian and Gay Mental Health: 1-800-547-7433)

Mental Illness

National Alliance for Mentally Ill: 1-800-950-6264

Pregnancy/Birth Control/STDs

Planned Parenthood (connects you with your local clinic): 1-800-230-7526
Emergency Birth Control: 1-800-584-9911
National STD Hotline: 1-800-1-227-8922
Sexually Transmitted Diseases Clinic: 1-810-573-2090
AIDS Hotline: 1-800-872-2497
Legal Guidelines for Age of Sexual Consent—click here

Rape/Sexual Assault

NO MEANS NO: 1-877-666-3267
RAINN—The Rape Abuse & Incest National Network: 1-800-656-4673

Runaway Services/Shelter

Family Youth Interventions: 1-810-758-7040
Runaway RAP Line: 1-800-292-4517

Smoking

Smoking Chamber of Horrors Web Site—click here

Suicide Prevention

National Youth Crisis Helpline: 1-800-999-9999
National Adolescent Suicide Hotline: 1-800-621-4000
Teen Suicide Prevention Hotline: 1-800-949-0057

Video Games, Television and Movies

"Video games are my life."
  -Boy, 14

This seems to be a very controversial issue between parents and their kids. On the one hand, some video games, TV shows and movies incite violence, limit creativity, and make it so kids never go outside to play anymore. On the other hand, some of the new generation electronic amusement toys can teach kids a lot about special relations and thinking tactics, and they can be educational and mind expanding.

I personally did not play video games growing up but watched a moderate amount of TV and movies. My brother, on the other hand, who was only one grade level above me, played video games all the time and constantly struggled with my parents to allow him to play more computer games, watch more movies, and see more television shows.

I really do believe there are positives and drawbacks for your children playing a lot of video games and/or watching a lot television and movies. The key is **balance.** Let's look at some of the pros and cons:

Video/Computer Games

Pros:

• Games can teach children to be adept at technology.

• Some games give kids good spatial recognition.

• Some games allow kids to think about tactical performance and work through clues to solve, build, or achieve a goal at the end of a game.

• Some games are educational and can teach kids everything from math to a foreign language to SAT vocabulary.

- They can play games with friends or siblings in their own home where supervision is possible. Games give kids something to do other than drugs, and they can do it with other kids in online

- Leadership and teamwork skills can be learned in running guilds.

Cons:

- Some games can incite violence.

- Playing games can discourage kids from playing outside or creating their own games.

- Playing games can make kids more solitary and not social if they only play computer/video games.

- Games may be extremely addictive and can cause withdrawal behaviors.

Television and Movies

Pros:

- Educational programming can teach your kids history, nature, moral lessons, and the arts.

- Watching movies and TV gives kids something to do other than drugs.

- Watching movies and TV can stimulate the imagination in different ways through stories and special effects.

- Watching movies and TV can enlighten kids about perspectives and lifestyles other than their own. They can make them feel less lonely when they see a character with whom they can relate.

Cons:

- Many movies and television shows are filled with violence, sex, and aggression which are dramatized, unrealistic, and inappropriate for kids and teens.

- Watching movies and TV can discourage kids from playing outside or creating their own games.

- Watching movies and TV can make kids more solitary and not social if they only watch television and movies.

My recommendation for parents is to have a balance among TV, video games, movies, playing outside, and non-electronic games. There also needs to be a limit on the types of programs kids are playing and watching.

Allow your kids to watch appropriate movies and television shows as well as buy them educational or non-violent computer and video games. Make sure they have a certain amount of time to go out with friends, play sports and relax, read or listen to music on their own. Especially encourage reading frequently because extensive reading really helps to build vocabulary, comprehension, and articulate speech. Reading also improves school performance and SAT scores later in high school.

Teenagers and Their Cars

"I fear the day my kid gets behind the wheel, not because I don't trust him, but because I don't trust anyone else."
  -Parent, 37

"Having a car will be the greatest. Having to ask my parents to drive me everywhere is a pain especially when they nag me all the way to my friends house"
  -Teenager, 15

For teenagers, cars mean freedom. For parents, cars mean fear. According to a Wall Street Journal article, "Insuring a Teen Driver for Less," the teen crash rate per mile driven is four times that of drivers older than 19. Lets face it, driving is dangerous for everyone and can be especially threatening when you combine underage drinking and driving. Most parents I interviewed said that they felt incredibly nervous about allowing their teenagers to drive, but they knew it was an inevitable part of growing up. For teenagers, driving gives freedom and allows teenagers to avoid having to rely on parents or car-pools for rides. On the other hand, teen driving can mean added costs with parking and gas as well as having to drive friends around. Parents have to deal not only with the added cost of a car, but they must also worry about what their teenager is doing with the newly found freedom.

I have a few suggestions for dealing with the car issue:

- My parents made me wash their cars every weekend starting when I was 12 to start paying off the car I would get at 16. When I was 12, my brother and I every Saturday morning would thoroughly wash and vacuum both of the family cars and log it into our computer. We got $10 per car in the log, and this went towards the final payment for the car. Thankfully, my parents covered the difference. I think this system was great because it made me work for the car I wanted. When I got it, I was very thankful and appreciative. Second, my parents did not have to wash the cars for a few years. Third, it taught us how to take care of our cars, and we stopped spilling food on the inside of our minivan because we knew we would be the ones who had to scrape it off on Saturday morning.

- Before even considering buying your teen a car, lay out some ground rules. Many teenagers assume that as soon as they get a car and get their license to drive, they will have freedom from curfew, can go to whatever party they want, etc. Make sure your teen understands from the early teen years that if they continue to keep your trust, a car will bring some new freedoms, but these will not be a complete break from all previous rules.

- Be good examples! If you do not want your child talking on the phone while driving, then don't do it yourself. Always wear your seatbelt! Try to make a point of being a cautious driver so that your kids can learn how to drive correctly.

- Many parents asked me what age I recommend to allow kids to start driving and going out with their friends. Honestly, this depends on your teenager and the amount of trust you have with them.

Teens: You need to build trust with your parents so that when you are able to drive, they will allow you to do so.

Parents: You need to honestly assess the amount of trust you have in your teen when setting up the rules of the road for them. Being too strict will alienate them, while being too lenient can give them too much freedom to be reckless.

- Cutting the cost:
  1. Ask insurance companies if they offer discounts for good grades.
  2. Ask insurance companies if they offer discounts for taking safety courses.
  3. When insuring family vehicles for your teen, put your teen on the vehicle that is less expensive to insure.
  4. You can try to trim excess collision and comprehensive coverage.

PART IV

Teenage Interaction

"The rules of my high school are like unwritten law, you don't go sit with the computer nerds, if you want to be cool."
 -Male, 16

The rules that guide teenage interaction are becoming increasingly more complex and difficult for parents and even teenagers themselves to understand. Being popular, having a boyfriend, being invited to a party, what you wear, and who you hang out with all become the focal points for the lives of many high schoolers and middle schoolers today. It is impossible for me to try to explain the intricacies of the teenage interaction to parents or the secrets of being popular to teenagers. However, it is crucial for both parents and teens to understand that teenage relationships are sensitive, fickle, and ever changing. I hope, by reading this section, parents will understand where their kids are coming from when they are moody or begging to go to a certain party, and that teenagers will realize that they are not alone in their need to be popular or avoid bullying or feelings of alienation.

Teenage Dating

"My parents do not let me date and I hate them for it because I am so left out and boys don't even talk to me."
  -Female, 16

"I know he hates it, but I don't think he is old enough to go out by himself yet, we have to chaperone on dates"
  -Mother

Dating in general is tricky, heartbreaking, fun, depressing, intimidating, and much more. When it comes to teenage dating, the rules can change constantly, and new issues frequently arise. Dating, love, crushes, infatuations, and relationships are a big part of every teenager's life. It doesn't matter what school you go to, what sex you are interested in, what you do during your free time, or if your parents allowed you to look at the opposite sex or not, dating is a huge issue socially, emotionally, and physically.

For many teens, dating can be defined in different ways. If two people are dating it can mean any of the following:

a.   They are boyfriend and girlfriend in a closed relationship (cannot see other people).

b.   They are boyfriend and girlfriend in an open relationship (can see other people).

c.   They are two people who like each other and go out on dates, but are not in a physical relationship together.

d.   They are a two people on a blind date or on the first few dates to see if they like each other.

e.   They are two friends who go to the movies and dinner together, but don't have a physical relationship.

Depending on the people, the circumstances, and regional area, dating can mean any of those five things. I would like to explore some guideline rules for teenage dating. Everything varies from person to person. Dating is so ambiguous that when it comes to rules and commonalities, it is difficult to write about how dating works. Therefore, I decided to give some examples and an overview of teenage dating behavior as well as general knowledge about dating for all ages. It is especially important to recognize the differences between the sexes and the female/male wrong assumptions.

<u>Females versus Males</u>

One of the reasons people find dating so incredibly hard and intimidating is because of the difference in the way men and women think when it comes to dating and relationships.

In the book *Why Men Don't Listen and Why Women Can't Read Maps*, Barbara and Allen Pease discuss the physiological, physical, and emotional differences between men and women. Even though in today's society women have avoided certain stereotypes and have attempted to break free from traditional female roles, many of the physiological reasons women were originally put into those roles still hold true. Here is a small summary and sampling of the Pease's book, which is incredibly interesting and represents a huge breakthrough in the relations between men and women.

> **Women** tend to be more emotional and sensitive to their feelings and issues in their lives.

> **Men** use aggression and have been trained to hide their feelings instead of showing them.

> **Women** use their entire brain when they think about problems or issues.

> **Men** compartmentalize and only use specific areas of their brain intended for each task. This is why men cannot multi-task easily.

> **Women** need to talk to express their feelings.

> **Men** don't express their feelings at all. When they do, it is through something physical, such as sports, sex, or fighting.

> **Women** need to feel emotional commitment to have sex.

> **Men** just want to have sex.

After I read the book, my frustration with the opposite sex lessened, simply because I knew there was scientific evidence for the feud between the sexes. I realized besides the scientific differences in the way the male and female brains work, there are certain things men and women do, especially teenagers, to cause disaster.

The major cause of struggle when it comes to teen dating is that teenage male and teenage females make wrong assumptions about each other. Our generation (just as the ones before it) is very ignorant about the true differences between men and women. We drive ourselves crazy over it. Here are some of the major areas of anxiety for teenagers about relationships:

1) Girls fret; boys take it as it comes.

It is proven women often use more of their brain when thinking, speaking, and acting. Men, on the other hand, compartmentalize and usually use less of their brain because they only focus on doing one thing at a time. This constant thinking and brain activity also means girls usually overanalyze and weigh out possibilities much more than boys do. Even though this can have many advantages in other areas of a girl's life, when it comes to dating, it can be a girl's downfall. In relationships or even during the "crush" stages of an attraction, girls overanalyze every conversation, gesture, and interaction that they have with their crush or boyfriend. Boys usually do not count the number of times the girl says hello in the hallway or pay attention to who called whom first. Boys don't think about the tone of voice she used when she brought up the upcoming dance, and they don't monitor the key dates and anniversaries that mark the relationship.

Because girls tend to overanalyze, they also second guess themselves or think they are too obvious. Then they start living up to the stereotype of girls being hormonally psychotic, overly sensitive, or both. Boys are also often blamed for being too laid back. This is why so many boys think having a girlfriend who is high-maintenance is the end of the world.

- How to overcome this:

    The first point to realize for boys and girls is this overanalyzing by girls versus the easygoingness of boys is scientifically based. The way our brains work and how we have been trained to think for generations is physiologically part of our nature. So simply by understanding the differences between the sexes, teens can become less frustrated about miscommunications and differences in behavior. Another way to overcome this is for you and your boyfriend or girlfriend to talk about it. If a boy knows that it drives his girlfriend nuts when he gets off the phone abruptly, he needs to know that she gets upset because she thinks he is bored with her, when, in actuality, its 8:01 P.M., and he really wants to watch <u>South Park</u> on television. These seemingly small instances can either cause a fight all on their own or build up to a huge blow out. Lastly, a little compromise will go a long way. Girls need to understand that guys don't overanalyze things and usually don't mean to commit insensitive or acts which piss off their girlfriends. In other words, girls should analyze a little less and boys should take care to either explain some of their seemingly rude actions or pay attention to what pisses their girlfriend or girlfriends off.

2) Girls are overly emotional.

This tends to go along the same lines as girls who are overly analytical and paranoid, however, there are some major differences. No matter how insensitive a girl thinks she might be, she will always be more sensitive than every boy. Boys tend to be insensitive to girls' feelings while every girl craves a sensitive romantic boyfriend. (As a side note for boys: if you want to impress a girl, show your sensitive side.) Sensitivity to each others feelings is a huge fight starter, especially in teen relationships, because guys have not yet learned about the need to pay attention to the girl's feelings, and girls are usually even more sensitive as teenagers due to lower self esteem and hormones.

- How to overcome this:

  As I said before, being aware of the issue is the first step toward making it go away. If boys would simply keep in mind the susceptibility of girls and remember to be more careful and attentive to her feelings on a daily basis, not only would the girl be much happier with him, but there would also be many fewer fights. Girls need to remember boys usually don't mean whatever they said, did, or didn't do. Girls need to give their guys a little slack. Girls often forget to take that into consideration. (You may need to remind him of your grandma's birthday so he doesn't forget, your art show, or the fact that he needs to make reservations for Valentines Day.)

3) Boys don't even notice.

This applies to all kinds of dating, crushing, and teenage interaction. Boys do not notice. Girls do. Girls can think of a thousand and one ways to flirt with the guy in math class including a shorter skirt, dropping a pencil, asking for homework help, giving homework help, a study session suggestion, or even throwing your book. In the end, you usually have to tell the guy flat out that you like him or else he won't notice. I don't know how many times I liked a guy in eighth or ninth grade and then found out a few years later he liked me, too.

"But I flirted with you all the time," I said.

"Really? I never noticed," he responded.

This doesn't only apply to flirting but also to upset girlfriends, soon to be broken up relationships, and hints for birthday presents.

- How to overcome this:

  This advice goes mostly to the girls, but I do encourage boys to be more attentive to their girl counterparts or girls around them. The advice is for girls to SPEAK UP. If you like a guy, tell him. If you know what you want for an anniversary/birthday/holiday, tell him. If you are upset, tell him. And for goodness sake if you want to end a relationship, tell him. Don't hint around and wait and see if he gets it.

Dating Etiquette

Here is the summary of rules that teenagers themselves came up with during their interviews with me:

Dating Rules

1. Never date a friend's ex.

2. Never date a friend's crush (recent or old).

3. Never date someone of whom your friends do not approve.

4. Always date someone you could introduce to your parents.

5. Never become better friends with your boyfriend's or girlfriend's best friend than your boyfriend or girlfriend themselves.

6. Never call or purposely become close with the friends of your mate unless it was like that before the relationship.

The Explanations

1) Never date a friend's ex.

I made this the first rule of dating because it is very important. If you want to end a friendship, piss people off, or look like a complete traitor, date a friend's ex. Even if your friend says that they are over the person, there will always be feelings to get in the way.

2) Never date a friend's crush (recent or old).

The same explanation as above applies here, especially with girls. Going out or even liking someone else's current or old crush can be seen as an attempt to snub or be better than your friend. If you do try to date a friend's crush, you will not only end up ruining the friendship, but also the relationship between you and the crush will end up not working out.

3) Never date someone of whom your friends do not approve.

At first read this might sound shallow, but if you think about it, this makes a lot of sense. There are two reasons why this rule is important. The first is if you are close with your friends and value their opinions, there is probably a good reason why your friends do not approve of your desired boyfriend or girlfriend. Your friends also probably know you better than you think, and if they think the person is a bad person or the relationship won't work ... it probably won't.

4) Always date someone you could introduce to your parents.

I know teenagers read this rule and think, "You have got to be kidding me!" The truth is that most teenagers subconsciously date someone their parents would hate as a form of rebellion. It is important to date someone that your parents like, because it will make it easier when it comes to the actual dating. If they like him or her and trust you, they will let you see each other more often and make it easier to date. Also, even though teenagers do not like to admit it, your parents only want the best for you, and if they do not like your significant other, there is definitely a reason. There was only one person I dated that my parents didn't like. At first, I was angry and didn't understand why they didn't like him. After a couple of months I realized what a sketchy guy he was, and I wished I had taken my parent's advice. I swear that mothers have a sixth sense with these things.

5) Never become better friends with your boyfriend's or girlfriend's best friend than your boyfriend or girlfriend themselves.

This one can get kind of tricky, yet it is pretty self-explanatory. Follow it, and you will not get into trouble.

6) Never call or purposely become close with the friends of your mate unless it was like that before the relationship.

I know how tempting it is to become friends with your boyfriend's friends, because they can give you the inside gossip and speak highly about you to him, but a guy needs his space and his male friends. Let him have some of his own things. You should also have some of your own privacy in your life. I also know it is easy for a guy to become friends with his girlfriend's friends, because his girlfriend constantly talks about them and drags them out with the poor guy. Yet, be careful how close you get with them, because girls can get very jealous even when there is no real reason for the upset.

Overall dating can become a very sticky issue between the sexes and with friends. In my own life, I have had numerous fights over boys and about who is dating whom. All teenagers and parents should keep in mind what a sensitive issue dating is for everyone.

Dating Dangers with Friends

I used to get along great with my group of friends. We went out on the weekends, baked each other cookies on the holidays, and did simple things like called each other if someone was sick. They knew about everything in my life, and I knew about everything in theirs. In about ninth grade I began to date boys from other schools while many of them did not know any boys. because we went to an all-girls school.

At first, they were all were very excited for me and couldn't wait to meet my new guy friends and talk to me about who I liked. Then it became all about punishment. It got worse by the year as they felt that they were inadequate because they were not "with" someone. This is very telling about teenage dating: teenagers tend to date each other to show off or because that is what is cool to do. The fact my girlfriends did not know any boys had nothing to do with my friends' attractiveness or availability The reason they did not know boys was simply because they went to an all-girls school.

Many parents do not even realize how scarring teenage interactions can be. Friends can be cruel. Actions can be unforgivable, and teens rarely forget who was mean to them in high school, whether it was their best friend or the class bully.

Girls can be especially cruel, and this is one of the reasons many of my dating rules have to do with staying away from friend's crushes or ex's. Some girls can be very territorial with their men. Girls who are willing to cross into other's territory have to be very desperate and usually face serious consequences. Many teenagers become desperate to be "hooking up" or have a boyfriend or girlfriend because they are put into a teen culture where having members of the opposite sex attracted to you is crucial. This is why so many girls end up having sex so early—it makes them feel wanted.

Teenagers need to keep in mind they will have the rest of their lives to date, and probably have more successful relationships when the participants are older and more mature and parents aren't looming over a relationship's head. Parents should remember their own experiences and always give their kids support, knowing they are probably going through tough teenage interactions.

Teenage Interaction

The Group Syndrome

Commonly referred to as a clique, groupings of teenagers seem to plague and dominate the lives of most teens. The underlying rules of social interactions restrict the interaction among teenagers and place loads of pressure on the shoulders of high school and middle school students.

1. Everyone is in a group whether it is the "floater group" (those who travel around to different groups individually or with another), the "popular group", the "nerd group" or even "Chelsea's/Amy's/Scott's group".

2. The mixing of groups or the mixing of people within the groups is common but usually is the source of many problems. If a girl or boy wishes to switch cliques or even be friends with people in other cliques, the original group can become jealous or possessive. People in the new group may also become protective of their pre-established friends. The reason for this is group contents, mechanics, and members are pieces of established common knowledge. Switches in groups alter friendships, make enemies, and encourage gossip. The switches are usually characterized as "abandonment" in the sense that either the group is "abandoning" a certain person, or a single person is leaving or "abandoning" the group.

3. A person's group can limit or effect whom they date.

4. A person's group can limit or effect social activities, hobbies, and/or sports.

5. A person's group can influence behavior in both good and bad ways.

   Why is it that groups are so powerful among teenagers?

   The first reason is that the teenage years are such a vulnerable and difficult time that teenagers often "fall into" groups to make them feel more secure.

The actual definition of a group is defined in the Merriam-Webster's dictionary as:

Group: (*n*) a number of individuals related by a common factor, as physical association, community of interests, or blood.

Usually teens do find their groups through a common factor, such as a sport, class, or hobby. Yet, the cause of groups can actually be why they are so dangerous. Teenagers are so diverse individually that to have a group of friends based on a single interest or on a few common ones is deadly. First, finding a group based on a common hobby makes it harder for teenagers to experiment or do a variety of activities in their lives, which is normal. Second, if you end up not getting along with your friends who are in the same sport as you, and you have a falling out with those friends, it can jeopardize your participation and love for the sport.

Teenagers will inevitably change, since the teenage years are the biggest "change years" in a human being's life. Despite this inevitability, the group mentality is based in a sense and need for permanence. Keeping the same people in the group, keeping most others out, and maintaining the hierarchy of the group is crucial to a group's survival. This is why girls and boys can often be so brutal when it comes to singling people out or punishing outsiders.

If an individual in a group starts to be different or change things around, it is not uncommon for them to be cast out from the group. On the other hand, if someone tries to enter a new group, they will often be accused of abandoning their friends for other people. And those other people might have issues of their own in letting the newcomer into the group's pre-established hierarchy.

In this section so far, I have been talking in very general terms about cliques and groups. I, personally, could fill another book simply with horrible experiences I've had with cliques, as could most teenagers. I think the issues of friends and cliques do not go away, and the rules stay the same through almost all generations. In the next couple of pages I give personal stories of how I was hurt by the clique mentality. For more examples, sadly, watch *any* teen movie.

Group mentality and why groups can be so dangerous and so powerful.

Teenagers in a group can do a lot more harm roaming around on a Saturday night than a single teen or even a pair of teenagers can do. The reasons why groups and cliques are so attractive to most teenagers, despite the pain and hurt that surround them, are as follows:

1. Having a group to depend on means you will never be alone. Most teenagers have to deal with group hierarchy and cliqueiness instead of being ridiculed by many different cliques as a loner. Having a secure group of friends means you will usually have someone there to back you up.

2. Followers have a place and so do leaders. No matter what kind of person you are, follower, leader, or somewhere in between, there is a social spot for you in a group. You cannot follow a leader, be a leader, or act out any other role you believe represents who you are if you are by yourself or are attached at the hip to another loner.

3. The power factor is critical. It is much more intimidating to have a group of people come up to you asking for your homework, lunch money, or a ride home than if only one person approaches you. Being in a group gives you more power to act out because you have more than yourself pushing for a cause. Whether that cause is recruiting for the track team or doing routine lunch money raids, the more the merrier.

    Groups are not only more appealing power wise, but they can also be very dangerous. Most parents tend to think as long as their teenager goes to the party, mall, or game in a group, it will be much safer and, therefore, okay. This is not always true. Group mentality goes as follows:

*   There are two leaders of a group, and they are big drinkers. They decide on the way to the movies (with the support of three "yes-men") to buy some beer and drink it. Not uncommon. As the two leaders, three yes-men, and four followers drink, the leaders decide to have a race between the two cars that they are all riding in ... you know, to see whose car is faster, like in *Fast and the Furious*. (Teenagers really do this, by the way.) The followers of the group, who usually don't drink that much and definitely do not drag race, think this is a bad idea. However, with two leaders and three yes-men, they'd be wimps if they didn't play along and allow drunken car racing on city streets. Do you see where this is going?

So, sometimes when parents fall back on the saying "safety in numbers," maybe they shouldn't.

Bullying, Singling out, and Other Ways of Ostracizing Teens

Because of the power and dangerous mentality cliques hold, they easily bully others. We saw how extreme the effects of bullying and singling out can get at Columbine or through other school shootings. Cliques are brutal. Social pressures are extensive, and the need to be accepted can become deadly. That is why it is so important for teenagers and parents alike to realize how ridiculous some of the teenage rules are and to understand why people act the way they do. In the next section, I discuss some of the insensitivity and problems groups can have and how to deal with them.

It is important for parents to understand calling the mother of the bully to give the kid a piece of your mind or going to school to "tell the little brat what you think" will not help. Unfortunately, the most parents can do for their teenagers is to give them books like this so they understand that they are not alone and to let them know you are there for them.

Another great option is a set of videos called Bully 911 at www.Bully911.com.

The ways that teens ostracize their peers:

- Aggression: Complete physical intimidation or threatening is not uncommon in most high schools across the country and throughout the world. This is either by a single bully to an individual or a group of intimidators to another person.

- Passive Aggression: A favorite for girl cliques, this type of aggression is not only the most hurtful because it is <u>not</u> truly out in the open, but it is also the hardest to stop because it can be deniable. Passive aggressive behavior includes purposely not including someone in an event or a plan and then talking about the event that they missed, talking behind someone's back, or sabotaging plans and other relationships or accomplishments.

• Gossip is a type of passive aggression, but it really is its own category, because it is used as such a major way of hurting others. Whether the gossip is true or completely fabricated, it is always hurtful.

In the end, either teenagers graduate with the same group because they followed the rules, or they graduate with scarred memories and a lot of enemies. Of course, there are always people who seem never to have a problem with their group, and they are extremely fortunate and hard to find. Even those teenagers I interviewed who had enjoyed pretty good experiences with their friends had seen other fights or just happened to avoid them by choosing not to become involved or take offense.

Why Teenagers Fight

When asked about their memories of high school and their high school friends, many adults, especially the women, brought up the cattiness, cliquiness, and fighting. I do admit teenagers fight more often and more voraciously than some other age groups (besides young adults ages 9-12 years of age). I began to think about why this happened and came up with an explanation that seemed to make every teenager I told go, "Oh yeah!"

Unfortunately, teenagers have a problem listening. I am sure most parents can attest to the fact that not only do teenagers have trouble listening and admitting they are wrong, but they also are very good at actually turning off their hearing and acting completely uninterested toward any order, compliment, or story someone is telling. Despite what most parents believe, teenagers do this un-hearing trick with adults _and_ other teenagers.

I believe the problem of simple <u>miscommunication</u> between teenagers is actually the source of some major fights. Especially for girls, a misunderstood look, weird tone of voice, or signing off too quickly online can be misinterpreted as an insult, put down, or avoidance. How many times do you, as a girl, or as a boy, hear other girls say to each other:

"Are you mad at me? Are you sure you are not mad at me? Because you

a. walked out of math today without saying goodbye."

b. totally looked at me weird in the hallway before school."

c. didn't call me last night."

d. told me you didn't like my haircut."

e. used a 'mean' voice when you said goodbye yesterday."

I could come up with a thousand more of these examples that seem silly, but they are completely feasible reasons for girls to think someone is mad at them. Think about all of the movies showing teenage girls overanalyzing about how a guy said hello to them, how many times he called after "x" many days, or if he said "hey" or "wassup" on Instant Messenger. Sadly, girls do fret about these things when it comes to boys and girls. Most boys do not care or even think about whether there is any difference among "hello" or "yo" or "what's up" as a measure of anything when talking to girls.

Unfortunately, there is reason for girls to think a slight voice tone change, look, or hair toss is symbolic of an attitude change.

Because girls have been socialized to keep their anger inside, not show their feelings, and avoid any and all conflict. Because anger is not what girls should do, they learn to either hold everything inside or show their anger or feelings in smaller ways.

This is why girl "fights" can involve neither party knowing what they did wrong, but they both know something is up and are being punished for it. This is why girl fights can last so long—because no one is willing to talk about it or bring their feelings out into the open. Invariably, when a passive fight is finally brought up, neither girl knows why they were fighting. So many fights start because of simple miscommunication. If you don't really understand what I am trying to get at, let me give you an example. The major principles in this point are that girls have been accustomed to holding their feelings in, that they show little grudges in other ways, and when they overanalyze and try to read one of these gestures, they misinterpret them for anger, sadness, love and/or avoidance. A misinterpretation can turn into a huge blow-out fight over a couple of weeks or days.

Example: Sarah is friends with Lauren, and they are in a whole group of friends together. These friends eat lunch, hangout on the weekends, and shop together during their free time. Of course, there are girls in the group who are closer to each other than with all of the girls in the group, making pairs and triplets of best-best-friends in a group of best friends. (This is very common, by the way.) Sarah and Lauren are best-best friends. On the phone one day, Sarah comments to Lauren, laughingly, that she thinks Lauren's crush, Richard, is "kinda nerdy". They laugh about it and continue the conversation, hang-up, and agree to see a movie over the weekend. The next day in math class Lauren doesn't sit in the empty seat next to Sarah. Sarah wonders why, but thinks that maybe she wanted to sit with some other girls from their group. At lunchtime Sarah offers Lauren her daily after-lunch mint, and Lauren says, "No, thanks." Throughout the week, little interactions like this happen, and Sarah is miserable trying to figure out what she did wrong. She asks her mom, brother, and all of the other girls in the group if she knows if anything is wrong, but she never asks Lauren. By now, everyone in the group knows and is telling Lauren that Sarah is mad at her and has been talking about Lauren to everyone. Now Lauren, who was a little peeved before about the Richard comment, is really pissed because Sarah is talking behind her back. This goes on for about two weeks making both parties miserable and the whole group angry at each other because they have all picked sides. In the end there is almost a big falling out when it is realized that nothing was wrong in the first place, because Sarah was just teasing Lauren about Richard being nerdy. (By the way, Lauren stopped liking Richard last week.)

This story was incredibly and sadly easy for me to write because so many different variations of this happen every day at my high school as well as others. Variations can happen with the opposite sex.

Another thing this example shows is the inability to have confrontations for many teenagers, especially girls. Boys tend to either say their feelings outright to other boys or start a physical fight. Girls, on the other hand, have serious problems admitting they are wrong and confronting an issue especially if they think they are at fault. Again, girls were brought up to avoid confrontation and arguments. This habit alone can be the source of many overblown fights.

Keeping in consideration the problems with misinterpretations and hiding feelings, another issue is teenage callousness. This might sound odd, but once you think about it, you'll remember your own teen experiences, and that insensitivity and the cruelty teenagers portray can scar and hurt people. Racism, sexism, homophobia, and general prejudice come into play when looking at teen insensitivity. In the cases of slandering, bullying, insulting, and demeaning actions to people who are different than the prejudice and callous teens themselves, it is that insensitivity and cruelty that causes so many teen hate crimes.

As I said earlier, I could fill a book solely with my own experiences of cliques, but because so many teen movies feature this, and because anyone who has been or is a teenager could tell you, I will not go through more than a couple of my own examples of how callous and insensitive teenagers, especially teenage girls, can be to each other. Mostly teenagers are extremely self-centered. Here are some examples of how you, your child, or your friends can have difficulty with a teenager's callous self-interest.

a. Sarah is having a birthday party and invites everyone except one girl who sometimes eats lunch with her and her friends. Yet, they talk about the party all of the time up until the party and then for weeks after. No one ever acknowledges that one girl wasn't invited.

b. Three girls who are the best-best friends in a group are constantly going on weekend trips with each other, seeing movies, and having sleepovers while not including other people in the group. They talk about their outings all of the time, and when asked why others in the group weren't invited, they respond with, "We didn't know you wanted to come." Others are still not invited the next time.

c.   A couple of guys decide to go to a party that a friend is throwing on Saturday. They don't want one of their friends, Andrew, to come because he is a drag. They talk about it in front of him, but insist that it is invitation only while laughing about how he wasn't invited and definitely cannot come. He finds out after the fact that there were no invitations. He doesn't say anything.

It is this kind of cruelty and these kinds of interactions which cause crashes in self-esteem, suicide, drinking, drug use, or self-violence in teenagers.

Conclusion

The teenage parent relationship is a tumultuous one, but with work can be made better through mutual understanding. If both parents and teenagers work together to communicate better and trust more they will be able to bridge the generation gap. The teenage years should not be about survival, but rather be a period of happiness and growth.

Every relationship has good and bad times. No matter how much you try to understand one another, miscommunications will occur. Instead of being frustrated by the ups and downs of the relationship, understand that it is a process. Building a solid foundation during these formative years will make for better life-long relations.

I hope that this book was able to shed light on the issues between teenagers and their parents from a teenage perspective. To be honest, it only skims the surface of the dimensions in the transition from teendom to adulthood.

Soon we will be starting a seminar series for teenagers and their parents. These seminars will change the relationship between parents and teenagers forever. Check out our website for when a seminar is coming to your town.

www.YoureGroundedBook.com

Our website also has the most amazing resources for teenagers and parents. Weblinks for safe activities near you, online resources, and other **You're Grounded!** products that can take your relationship to the next level.

Quick Order Form

Fax Orders: 310-839-3636

Email Orders: vvanpetten@youregrounded.com

Postal Orders: Vanessa Van Petten, 10736 Jefferson Blvd #142, Culver City, CA 90230, USA

Please send the following books, disks or reports:

_____

_____

_____

Name:
Address:
City: State: Zip:
Telephone:
Email Address:

Sales Tax: Please add 7.75% for products shipped from California address

Shipping by Air:
U.S: $4.00 for first book or disk and $2.00 for each additional product.
International: $9.00 for first book or disk; $5.00 for each additional product (estimate).

978-0-595-43875-4
0-595-43875-X